HOW TO IMPROVE
CUSTOMER SERVICE

HOW TO IMPROVE YOUR
CUSTOMER
SERVICE

STEVE MACAULAY and SARAH COOK

KOGAN PAGE

First published in 1993

Apart from any fair dealing for the purposes of research or private study, or criticism or review, as permitted under the Copyright, Designs and Patents Act, 1988, this publication may only be reproduced, stored or transmitted, in any form or by any means, with the prior permission in writing of the publishers, or in the case of reprographic reproduction in accordance with the terms of licences issued by the Copyright Licensing Agency. Enquiries concerning reproduction outside those terms should be sent to the publishers at the undermentioned address:

Kogan Page Limited
120 Pentonville Road
London N1 9JN

© Stephen Macaulay and Sarah Cook, 1993

British Library Cataloguing in Publication Data
A CIP record for this book is available from the British Library.
ISBN 0 7494 0999 1

Typeset by DP Photosetting, Aylesbury, Bucks
Printed and bound in Great Britain by Biddles Ltd

◄ CONTENTS ►

Acknowledgements   *6*
Introduction   *7*

Part 1. Managing the Customer Interface   11

1. Customer-focused Leadership 12
2. Creating a Positive Image with Customers 19
3. How to Deal Assertively with Customers 27
4. Managing the Problem-solving Process 35
5. Positive Persuasion and Negotiation 42
6. Total Quality Management 51
7. Dealing with Difficult Customer Situations 57

Part 2. Leading Your Team Resourcefully   63

8. Communication and Getting the Message Across 64
9. Teamwork 80
10. Recruitment and Selection 89
11. Performance Management 98
12. Training and Development 112
13. The Internal Customer 126

Part 3. Managing Yourself   131

14. Developing Yourself 132
15. Time Management 142
16. Managing under Pressure 153

Conclusion   *164*
Bibliography   *167*
Index   *171*

◀ ACKNOWLEDGEMENTS ▶

Special thanks to the many colleagues and associates who contributed ideas and encouragement for the development of this book. In particular Chris Blakeley, Peter Boggon, John Brindley, Meryl Court, Alison Gibb, Nigel Harding, Matthew Hind, Roger Pringle, Stefan Sjöstrom, Tracy Smith, Lars Turndal, Peter Wilson and Mike Westwood, and, through their example, David Taylor and Una Richens who have provided a positive role model of customer service management at its best.

◀ INTRODUCTION ▶

The marketplace is becoming more competitive, and it is no longer possible to run a business without a very strong focus on the customer. Achieving this focus can appear to be an expensive matter, adding to managers' ever-increasing problems of maximising use of their resources. Yet it must be done if the business is to succeed and, if it is done well, the rewards both for you, the businessperson, and the customer can be enormous.

This then is the management challenge of the '90s and beyond. How will you lead your team to provide an outstanding quality of service, and at the same time make efficient and wise use of resources? It is a tricky balancing act.

This book indicates the opportunities to be grasped when you get it right. It addresses the key questions that need to be asked, and guides you towards answers which are appropriate and useful for your business.

ARE YOU REALLY CUSTOMER CENTRED?

Many organisations who serve the customer spend a lot of their time looking inwards, and are organised accordingly. They see the customer as being removed from them, as in Figure I.1.

The truly customer-centred organisation has taken the trouble to think through what sort of procedures and structures work best for the customer. This puts the customer at the very centre of the organisation, as in Figure I.2.

Put the customer at the very centre of your organisation.

Which figure best fits your company today? Whatever the answer, let's look at how you can develop and strengthen your position as a customer-centred organisation.

8 INTRODUCTION

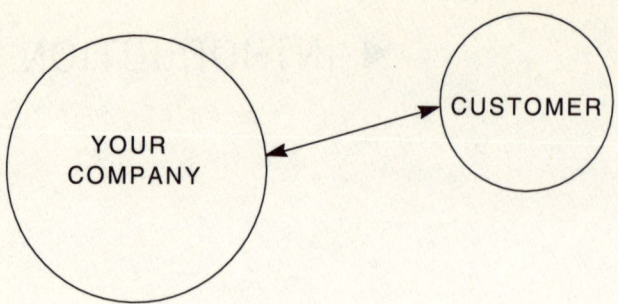

Figure I.1 *The inward-looking company*

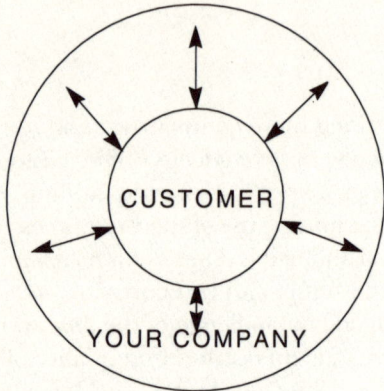

Figure I.2 *The customer-centred organisation*

SEIZING THE INITIATIVE

Leadership is much talked about in serving the customer, and with good reason, because leadership is about seizing the initiative, making it happen, and staying ahead as the world changes around you. A leader who lives and breathes customers' needs and communicates his or her vision with energy and vigour is an essential factor in developing service success.

He or she guides the team and directs individual efforts, steers events and sets a positive example to others. We are not talking of the abilities of a superstar here. The successful leader combines sureness in pursuing direction with the application of some thorough disciplines, in the following areas.

The successful manager is not a superstar but someone who sets a positive example.

- Managing the customer interface. Dealing with customers from reception through to invoicing so that the customer sees your organisation as totally positive and responsive.

- Leading your team. The art of creating disciplined energy to forge an unshakeable bond with the customer.
- Managing resources. Deploying all your resources – your people, systems, environment, finances – wisely.
- Managing yourself. Being self aware, at ease with yourself, constantly developing, competent in management of your time and priorities, dealing well with the pressures of the service culture.

MANAGING THE CUSTOMER INTERFACE

The image a company displays to its customers is reinforced or eroded through its day-to-day service contacts. These can be steered positively through:
- Developing and maintaining customer-friendly procedures which are relevant and not complicated or time consuming
- Solving problems incisively and creatively
- Handling customers skilfully, even in difficult situations.

LEADING YOUR TEAM

Creating a high achieving team involves you in the following processes of team and resource management.
- Communication. The disciplines of keeping everyone in the picture.
- Teambuilding. Working to maintain the right balance of contributions and keeping up energy and commitment.
- Spotting talent and developing it.
- Steering change. Recognising the need for change and then leading everyone along with you through the change process.
- Creating the right conditions for performance, including setting objectives and giving feedback, and payment and incentive methods which give a fair reward for effort and achievement.
- Managing all your resources, including people, information and money. Astute managers keep control by forecasting and keeping track of their business performance.

MANAGING YOURSELF

Customer service environments are often pressured, sometimes stressful places, but they can provide a wealth of personal development opportunities. The manager in such a situation needs stamina and an alert and positive outlook on life. This requires self-awareness and the ability to practise the techniques of time and stress management. Customers and colleagues notice and appreciate these characteristics.

HOW THIS BOOK WILL HELP YOU MEET THE SERVICE CHALLENGE

This book is a comprehensive improvement strategy for sharpening the service you deliver to the customer.

Each chapter takes you through an outline of the essentials of its topic area and relates the issues closely to meeting customers' needs. You will find practical guidelines, exercises and action orientated improvement tasks to help you develop a plan of action. The book will give you the basis for a comprehensive improvement strategy to sharpen the service you deliver to the customer.

Your strategy will be easier to put together if you jot down in a notebook your key learning points as you go along.

◀ PART 1 ▶
MANAGING THE CUSTOMER INTERFACE

◀ CHAPTER 1 ▶

CUSTOMER-FOCUSED LEADERSHIP

This chapter seeks to answer these questions:
- What is customer-focused leadership?
- What qualities and behaviours are required of a successful leader who serves the customer?
- How do you shape up as a leader?
- How can you develop your leadership skills?

WHAT IS A CUSTOMER-FOCUSED LEADER?

A leader is someone who provides inspiration and direction for a team and instils it with commitment to meeting customer needs. This involves:
- Guiding a team and concentrating individual efforts on the customer
- Taking the initiative and making things happen
- Being a source of motivation and an example to others.

Leadership is evident both in what you do and in the effect you have on other people.

In a customer service environment good leadership should be evident in what you do and in the effect on other people: staff, colleagues and above all customers. These effects include the following:
- Positive helpful attitudes to customers from all those who work with you
- Clear objectives which have the customer as an absolute priority
- A team all pulling together to serve the customer
- People who obviously have the ability to deal with customers speedily and knowledgeably
- Anticipation and planning ahead, so that the customer feels a sense of alert readiness to help

- Customer-friendly procedures – doing business in straightforward, not awkward, time-consuming or frustrating ways
- Flexibility to respond to change; foreseeing changing customer needs.

MANAGING AND LEADING

Leadership is more than day-to-day management. Leadership is about providing that extra something to move things forward with urgency, clarity and commitment. Positive things happen as a result of good leadership. Many managers know what they *should* be changing, but somehow they never find the time to do it. Leaders follow through energetically so that they and their teams are successful.

The formidable pressures of a changing world mean the successful manager needs two related skills:
1. The ability to keep a grip on the present and manage a steady state; this needs clear objective setting and planning and control mechanisms
2. The ability to excite, motivate and gain commitment to making progress and implementing change.

The first skill is usually that defined as management, and much of this book is devoted to management disciplines essential to manage a business tightly and make best use of resources. But this alone will not ensure success. A successful service organisation is constantly changing and improving. This requires leadership, the 'oomph' factor which a leader provides, and the following qualities:
- A vision of the future, an agenda for change
- Motivation, for the team to succeed
- Development of teamwork, commitment and loyalty, so that the team works hard to turn the vision into a reality.

How you provide these varies from organisation to organisation. It is a tough task which many find difficult to achieve, but for the sake of prosperity and long-term survival, managers must rise to the leadership challenge. Leadership is not just the prerogative of one powerful person at the top of an organisation; it needs to pervade all parts of a company.

TAKE ME TO YOUR LEADER

You may well be asking, 'Am I a leader or a manager?' A leader has developed a strong combination of the following qualities, skills and approaches:
- Good working relationships; a strong network of willing followers and

active supporters among colleagues, managers and customers, so that jobs get done and relationships are not just cosy
- Exceptionally strong interpersonal skills which earn respect and cooperation both within the team and with other departments inside the organisation, and outside the company with customers
- Credibility through a track record of accepting responsibility and delivering sound decisions
- Communication of a high level of energy and motivation; willingness to take the reins of responsibility and take risks to achieve progress rather than hang back for fear of possible failure
- A strong set of personal values and a mission which is communicated to others and inspires them.

A manager who is not a leader does not display all these qualities and characteristics. Managers are more likely to rest on the formal authority of their positions, their specialist job knowledge, or the narrower confines of their roles. Managers
- follow, and do not actively question, directions
- accept rather than eagerly grasp challenge and responsibility
- go for the obvious tasks rather than the difficult ones, the straightforward relationships rather than the thorny but potentially productive ones
- work within existing boundaries and their own team rather than within the whole organisation and outside it with customers.

This is not to write off management skills. It is vital to have implementers who will control and deliver. But they are skills of managing a steady state, rather than pushing ahead.

LEADERSHIP CHECKLIST

Use Table 1.1 to rate yourself on your effectiveness as a leader and champion of customers.

Table 1.1 *Leadership checklist*

An effective leader in a customer service environment:	Good	OK	Room for Improvement
Sees the customer as overwhelmingly the most important priority and lives by this priority every minute of the day			
Communicates a vision of the future – how to make the team number one in the eyes of the customer			
Sets clear objectives with team. No one is left wondering about priorities in serving the customer			

Table 1.1 *Leadership checklist* (contd)

	Good	OK	Room for Improvement
Inspires and creates a positive example of 'going the extra mile for the customer'			
Provides help, encouragement and support to the team as its members serve the customer			
Respects other people in the company			
Respects the customer			
Maintains a sense of customer focus even when under pressure			
Takes tough decisions even when it makes life difficult for a while			
Is honest about mistakes and open to feedback and comment			
Communicates effectively both with customers and with those inside organisation			
Trains and develops staff			
Recognises improvement possibilities and makes change happen			
Is committed to developing him or herself, the team, the department and the organisation			

CAN LEADERSHIP SKILLS BE DEVELOPED?

Yes! Leadership is built on sound management skills. No leader will succeed if the edifice of his or her management competence is crumbling. Leadership involves seizing the opportunities that are given to you. To achieve this you have to:

- Clarify your values
- Communicate your mission and goals
- Train others and implement a delegation plan
- Hold meetings, formal and informal, with customers and colleagues outside your team to stay in touch
- Clarify and manage your priorities
- Develop good information systems, formal or informal.

16 MANAGING THE CUSTOMER INTERFACE

THINK CUSTOMER, CUSTOMER, CUSTOMER

A customer-focused leader must keep the customer in mind at all times and encourage other people to do the same through his or her infectious energy, clear vision and actions. Try the following.

- Keep reminding yourself and everyone in the company how important it is to be helpful and responsive to the customer. In this way the customer will see the company in terms of the high quality service it provides. Do this by putting customer issues on the agenda at every communications meeting, publicising stories of successes in helping the customer, and feed back positive comments which customers make about your staff.
- Foster the sort of attitude where nothing is too much trouble for the customer. This means regularly reinforcing this message at team meetings. It means setting up procedures which avoid 'roadblocks' for the customer and allow speedy resolution of difficulties.
- Be consistent in your concern for customers – make this your top priority. Your people will remember the exceptions you make. Ensure there are none.
- Be positive and supportive to front line customer contact staff – their job can sometimes be a thankless one.

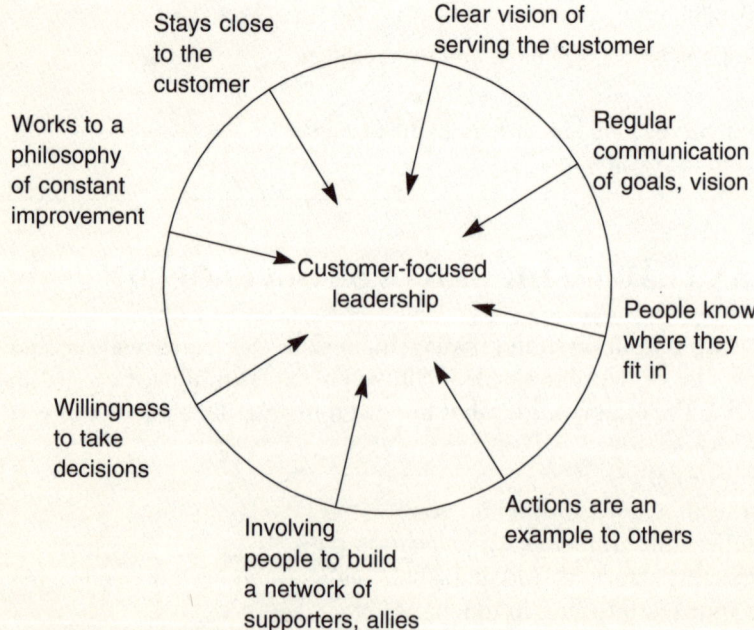

Figure 1.3 *Customer-focused leadership*

CUSTOMER-FOCUSED LEADERSHIP 17

SUMMARY

Leaders make a noticeable difference to customer satisfaction. They make things happen because they:
- Guide and focus their team
- Take the initiative
- Provide an example to others
- Energise everyone who delivers service
- Change things for the better.

They achieve this because they place the customer number one on their list of priorities and make sure everyone else in the organisation does too. They are the example others look up to. They also:
- Provide a vision for tomorrow, but provide guidance and clear objectives for today
- Work hard to support their people and treat them with respect
- Keep finding ways to do things better.

HOW TO INCREASE YOUR CUSTOMER-FOCUSED LEADERSHIP EFFECTIVENESS

Draw up your own list of important customer focused leadership characteristics. Start by thinking of someone you admire. What does he or she do which singles them out? Then work through the following points.

1. Look at the leadership qualities outlined in the checklist on page 14. List those positive qualities you bring to your team. Identify those areas where you need to improve. Set yourself a plan of action for developing these qualities.
2. Ask your staff what qualities they expect of you as a leader and how well you match their expectations. You could do this by a questionnaire followed up by a discussion with your team or, perhaps, through asking your team to make short presentations on this subject, followed by discussion.
3. Develop a vision for your company or department. Get your colleagues together and invite them to look positively at the future, assuming you all really work together as a strong team. Assess how you could best communicate this vision and make it a living reality.
4. Write down the goals and objectives of your team to meet this vision. Make certain these are specific and clear to everyone in the team. Check that these include both long and short term objectives. Regularly review how well you are performing against these objectives and recognise progress. Set yourself personal goals.
5. Raise issues about customers to your manager, colleagues and staff at every opportunity. Ensure you have frequent customer contact. Review the number of times you visit customers and set yourself an ambitious target to increase this.
6. Set yourself a goal to increase by at least 100 per cent the number of times you recognise the

achievements of your staff – a 'well done' and 'thank you' have a powerful motivating effect. Consider new ways to reinforce success in those around you.
7. Review how well you communicate with your team, with other people in the organisation and with people outside the organisation such as customers and suppliers. Assess ways you could invigorate this process to capture interest, win support and provide motivation.
8. Canvass the opinions of all those people with whom you and your team come into contact. See how you and your team can improve. Set a specific plan for improvement with your team. Lead the way for implementing change by making some visible personal changes. Review with your staff progress in achieving improvements.
9. Establish the values you believe are important in your company or department. Ask other people for their opinions outside the department or company. Publish a statement of the department's or company's values. Invite discussion on how to further these values. Develop a charter of customer rights and employee responsibilities with your team or other managers within your organisation. Identify ways to use training and development to reinforce the company's values and bring about change for the better in the way you serve the customer.

◀ CHAPTER 2 ▶
CREATING A POSITIVE IMAGE WITH CUSTOMERS

This chapter looks at:
- How you best project a positive image in a service environment
- The implications of developing a positive image and approach
- What you need to do to ensure you achieve a consistently positive image
- How you conduct skilful social relationships with customers
- How you should manage the work environment with the customer in mind.

Customers want to deal with organisations who recognise and go out of their way to satisfy their needs and expectations. A good service has three components, all of which enhance the image the organisation projects. These are:
1. The quality of the product or service you are providing
2. The way you go about delivering that service
3. The relationships that are formed person to person in providing a service to the customer.

Customers are influenced by the relationships they form with people in your organisation as well as your service quality and delivery.

WHAT IS MEANT BY A POSITIVE IMAGE

Creating a positive image means:
- Helping the customer to see the strengths of your products and in the best possible light
- Ensuring that you have done everything possible to engender a bright, positive impression of your organisation and its service during the delivery of your service
- Developing a relationship with customers that makes them feel special, valued and respected as individuals.

All this is a very subjective, individual process for each customer. Reputations, however, can be consciously built up. Each contact with the customer is a 'moment of truth' which contains the potential for a downward spiral of failure or an upward spiral to a productive relationship. It is easy to leave the development of this relationship to other people, such as sales people or marketing staff, and get on with the 'real business' of solving immediate service problems. But there are risks in a service environment for a manager who ignores or down plays image and reputation. Everyone plays a part in building the image of the organisation.

We can all think of examples where we would or would not buy a product or deal with an organisation, simply because we have had strongly positive or negative experiences. To see how powerful reputation is, try listing a few organisations who provide a service and give a one-line response on the quality of the service you believe they are likely to provide. For example:

Organisation	*Your view of service quality*
Inland Revenue	
Post Office	
Rolls-Royce	
BBC	
Marks and Spencer	
Your local garage	
British Rail	

Imagine what your customers would write if they completed this chart with your organisation at the top of the list. What does this say about the image you have developed?

Reputations build up over time and are slow to change. As a manager, your task is to ensure that every time you deliver a service to a customer you are creating a positive image of the organisation.

BUILDING UP AN IMAGE

People deal with people. The way the organisation comes across to others is largely through its staff. Researchers say that in most situations, more than 50 per cent of the personal impact we make on others is not dependent on what we say but on the way we say it and, in face-to-face situations, what we look like. As a manager, you need to review the impact you and your staff have on customers in such areas as:
- How you sit or stand – alert or slouching?
- Facial expressions – tired, frowning, or eager to help?

- Liveliness, helpfulness – energetic, ready to listen or dull and bored?
- Clothes, hairstyle – appropriateness for the situation?
- The friendliness or clarity of what you say – offering help or blocking it?
- The environment the customers find themselves in – for example background noise, cramped untidy reception, or comfortable chairs, literature to read.

To identify areas for improvement, you could get your team together and review under each of these headings things that are working well, and those aspects that create a negative impression. As a result you can draw up a team improvement plan.

Example
A colleague went to a bookshop in London last week and bought two books. The layout of the store was clear and invited you to pick up the books and buy them. The stock was extensive. However, at no time when he paid for his books did the assistant make eye contact. The only utterance he made was '£17.29'. Not once did he say 'thank you' or 'please' or 'sign here' or 'goodbye'. By this simple omission, the assistant had destroyed all the positive impression which had been built up.

Good reputations take time to build up but can be easily destroyed.

WRITTEN COMMUNICATION WITH CUSTOMERS

As well as personal contact, the way an organisation communicates with its customers in written format also creates a positive or negative image of an organisation.

Firstly, look at your company's corporate identity. Does this fit the image you would want it to project? Is your logo eye-catching and in keeping with your corporate values?

Next, look at the tone of your correspondence with customers and the manner in which it is written. How customer friendly is it? Is it written in a style which is too formal or too informal? Is the literature and product information you supply to customers accurate and up to date?

THE CUSTOMER ON THE TELEPHONE

The way in which an organisation responds to the customer on the telephone creates a powerful image of the organisation. Make sure that your phones are answered in a friendly and clear manner and that a greeting and company name are given.

Ensure that the people answering your telephones know where to direct calls and that your telephone directory is up to date. Make sure that all calls are answered and that the customer is not passed from pillar to post as this creates a poor image of an organisation.

If you are not certain how well your customers are handled on the telephone, make a personal call to your organisation to see how you are treated.

Try ringing up some of your competitors and assess how well they are faring in building their image through the telephone. Feed back any useful learning points to your team.

THE USE OF NAMES

Customers like to feel their business is important to the organisation. One way to create a positive image with customers is to know and use their names in your dealings with them.

Likewise, remember to let customers know your name as a point of contact for them. Remember to give the customer your business card on first meeting. Where possible, establish the names of the people who work with your customers such as secretaries, telephonists, assistants and work colleagues so that you can create a friendly and positive impression on these people too.

TIPS FOR IMPROVING YOUR IMAGE

Regular consistent attention to the whole process of contact with customers is necessary. Bear in mind the following.

- The power of the first few minutes. You will get off to a good start in a relationship with the customer by your initial greeting, and your approach in the first few minutes. Get off on the wrong foot and it takes a lot to correct, not just in that meeting but in future.
- Do not keep people waiting. This builds up frustration. If appropriate, offer the choice of ringing them back if it is a phone call, or calling back.
- Make a determined effort to be personable and friendly at all times; for example, say 'Good morning/Good afternoon'. Use the customers' names.
- Treat each customer as if they were the first of the day.
- In face-to-face situations, look at the customer.
- Smile, even when you are on the phone. It will show.
- In dealing with the customer, do not judge him or her (eg 'You shouldn't have done it that way', 'You shouldn't have let the agreement lapse').
- Communicate clearly, in words the customer understands.
- Make sure your written communication is clear and customer friendly.
- Avoid getting so overloaded that your attention is not on that customer.
- Find something genuine to say which is positive about the customer.
- Take trouble to satisfy the customer, even if this means going to extra trouble.
- Check your paperwork and literature. What impression is this creating? Could it be improved?

- Conduct regular campaigns to ensure customer standards are achieved and maintained.
- Comment on the way your staff deal with the customers as a regular part of performance review.
- Set service standards which specify what you expect of your staff. Agree these with them. Examples of service standards are:
  - Answer 'phone within three rings
  - Deal with correspondence the same day
  - Offer customers waiting in reception a coffee
  - Drive clean company vehicles
  - Always carry a business card and offer to new customers.
- People who feel good about themselves will feel good about their customers, and it will show. Take steps to encourage a bright positive team atmosphere where team members respect and appreciate each other. See Chapter 9 on teamwork for suggestions.
- Encourage your staff to visit customers and customers to visit you so that your people find out for themselves what their customers want and need, and build up good relationships with them.
- The power of ending on a high note. Summarise your actions. Check out that the customers' needs are fully met. Offer to be available for further help should they wish.

MANAGING SOCIAL RELATIONS WITH CUSTOMERS

A further aspect of creating a positive image with customers is how you deal with them on a social level.

Wining and dining

Many managers who deal with customers find themselves in social gatherings; for example hosting a buffet for a new product launch, taking foreign visitors out for a meal, entertaining regular customers during a working lunch. These events are an essential part of business life and help to win and keep customers, yet many managers feel uncomfortable in such settings. They may say: 'I hate making small talk', 'I always feel awkward at business do's', 'How can I eat and do business at the same time?', 'I'm sometimes not sure I'm doing or saying the right thing' or 'I'd rather avoid mixing business and pleasure'. Alternatively, many managers never give the matter a moment's thought.

To achieve success in work related social gatherings, you will rarely, if ever, need the elaborate correctness of Debrett's or a Swiss finishing school. But you do need to obey generally accepted standards and to recognise that social gatherings in business are another form of customer service in a different setting.

The opportunities of getting together socially
Social gatherings provide a chance to get to know the customer or prospect

outside the more restricting business framework, to find out more about their likes and dislikes, hobbies and interests. This allows you to address their needs with greater knowledge. Also, such gatherings allow you to present a less formal and narrow side as a company representative. The customer can see the company in a more personal and individual way. With established customers, informal occasions allow progress to be made on some issues which may have been more difficult in a formal setting. With prospects they allow the ice-breaking phase to be shortened.

Preparation beforehand
If we regard social gatherings as business meetings with some big potential benefits, we should consider beforehand:
- Why am I entertaining this customer?
- What do I hope to achieve?
- What are the implications of my behaviour?

It will help if you then do some homework and answer these questions:
- Are the venue, timing and seating appropriate for the customer?
- Do I need to ensure confidentiality?
- Have I allocated an appropriate amount of time?
- Am I operating within my budget?

COMPANY IMAGE CHECKLIST

Use this checklist to review the image you create with your customer.

Telephone answering
- Speed
- Quality
- Switchboard and extension standards
- Number of times callers are re-routed
- Message taking
- Telephonists' organisational knowledge.

Reception
- Greeting
- Speed of response
- Area comfortable, tidy, interesting
- Area free from noise, distractions
- Receptionist's knowledge of who's who.

Paperwork
- Literature

- Orders
- Invoices
- General correspondence
- Other.

Written/verbal communication
- Response times
- Easy to understand
- Details correct
- Face to face – friendly, helpful, professional
- Professional skills and knowledge displayed
- Company knowledge.

Customer contacts
- Frequency
- Quality of relationships built.

Follow ups
- Do we tie up all loose ends on contacts?
- How do we fare – letter/face to face?

Meetings
- On time, details confirmed
- Participants prepared
- Hospitality level
- Do we effectively manage time (our own and our guests)?

Company structure
- Visibility to customers
- Clarity of organisation
- Who's who.

Corporate identity
- Consistency between individuals and departments
- One company image.

General customer awareness of our business
- Employee knowledge.

Location/access directions
- Clear maps and directions
- Suggested routes easy to follow for visitors.

Site signs
- Clear
- Accurate
- Easy to follow.

Working environment
- Visitors are acquainted with fire procedures where appropriate
- Customers are not exposed to health and safety hazards.

SUMMARY

- Ensure that the way you deliver service to the customer portrays the organisation in a positive light. It is the regular service contact which provides the most powerful impression for many customers.
- Remember that people buy from people and ensure that your personal contact on a business and a social level with customers creates a good impression. Plan ahead to make the most of each meeting.
- Regular, consistent attention to the whole process of contact with customers is necessary to keep up standards.

EXERCISES

1. Put yourself in the place of your customers. Look at the image your organisation creates from the customers' viewpoint. Identify areas of agreement with your team, then decide what you can do to enhance the positive points and minimise the negative ones.
2. Consider conducting a survey on the image and reputation of your organisation. How visible is the company? How strongly are your good points known to customers? Do different groups perceive you differently? What are the implications for this?
3. Consider running a training course on how to project the company's image. Set up role-play situations and give feedback to those involved on how well they have communicated the company image.
4. Review each point of contact with customers and identify improvements. Use the checklist as a starting point to develop your own list, which can be used in regular service reviews.
5. Spot-check how well your organisation's health and safety procedures are known and followed and how these impact on the customer.

◀ CHAPTER 3 ▶

HOW TO DEAL ASSERTIVELY WITH CUSTOMERS

In this chapter we will consider:
- What assertiveness is
- How you distinguish it from other ways of dealing with customers
- What the benefits are
- How you behave assertively in difficult customer situations.

Assertiveness is important in customer service. You need to put your point over clearly, but nevertheless respect the customer and maintain a climate of good relationships.

To demonstrate how important assertiveness is, you only have to look at situations where you are not treated assertively. Not being assertive can, for example, spill over into being downright rude or curt, to someone timidly accepting blame when it is not their fault and failing to give their organisation a good image.

WHAT IS ASSERTIVENESS?

Assertiveness means putting over your point of view clearly and concisely while still respecting the rights and feelings of the other person – customer, colleague or boss for example. You can distinguish this from non-assertive behaviour which is essentially passive. Someone with aggressive behaviour puts their point over forcibly but is no respecter of other people's rights and feelings.

Let us take an example. A passenger at an airport complains at the check-in desk. He has arrived too late and cannot get a seat on the plane as it is full. He insists he be allowed on board. The booking clerk has to tell him he cannot fly on this plane and he will have to wait two hours for the next flight. An

Assertiveness means putting over your point of view clearly and concisely while still respecting the rights and feelings of the other person.

aggressive response from the booking clerk in this situation would be something like: 'Look, I've told you the situation. Can't you read the terms and conditions? You should have checked in on time. The plane's full'.

A non-assertive approach would be: 'I'm awfully sorry. Perhaps someone won't turn up at the last minute. I must have overlooked your booking on the computer. I'm ever so sorry, I didn't realise. I can't get anything right today'.

An assertive response would go something like this: 'I appreciate your frustration and I can see how urgent it is. I hope you'll understand that we can only reserve seats until a certain time. I'm sorry you are inconvenienced. Perhaps Air United could help you. They have a flight in 35 minutes'.

Who would you rather deal with? Almost certainly the one who responds assertively. You will not feel entirely happy, but you will feel the company representative understands the position and that you have been given a fair hearing.

HOW ASSERTIVE ARE YOU?

Do you more often than you would like find yourself:
- Getting angry because of poor cooperation from other departments
- Feeling powerless and unable to influence the decision makers
- Unable to answer back appropriately if someone puts you down
- Overwhelmed and unable to say 'no' when you're too busy
- Having your self-esteem and self confidence lowered by your dealings with customers?

THE BENEFITS OF ASSERTIVE BEHAVIOUR

An organisation has to set limits and put over bad news at times, but how you do it makes a vital difference.

Assertiveness is a way of behaving with other people which allows you to put your case over and do yourself justice without being overbearing. This is exactly what you need in many customer service situations. Any organisation has to set limits or put over 'bad news', but how you put it over can make a vital difference.

Assertiveness allows customer services representatives to feel comfortable with themselves. They have put a case over clearly and explained the company approach, but they have stayed courteous and professional throughout.

An aggressive approach would almost certainly lead to a poor image for the organisation. As a customer you only deal with aggressive customer service staff if you have to, and if there is a choice of companies you may well go elsewhere.

Compliant, non-assertive behaviour looks on the surface very customer orientated – it seems to give the customers what they want. In fact, since some limits have to be set in organisations, this position is not very tenable. It leads to an inconsistent approach and a weak sense of purpose.

THE ASSUMPTIONS NECESSARY FOR ASSERTIVENESS

In dealing with customers in an assertive manner we make the following assumptions:
1. You have a right to put over your case fully, and the customer has a corresponding right and expectation to be heard.
2. Mistakes should not overwhelm you – we all make some errors. Do not dwell on them. It is sorting out the future that matters most.
3. You can attain an appropriate balance between expressing your own views and feelings and listening to and respecting what the customer has to say.
4. Being assertive will not ensure the argument will come down in your favour, but it will increase the likelihood both parties will feel OK to do business in the future.
5. Assertiveness is a set of skills, but also reflects understanding, confidence and feeling positive about ourselves and other people.

A SHORT GUIDE TO BEING ASSERTIVE

1. Clarify your objectives. Go into a situation clear about where you want to go and what your priorities are.
2. Hear the other person out fully. This may take some while but it is worth it in terms of improved understanding and for the flow of rational conversation.
3. State your position and do not get too easily interrupted or deflected. Summarise if necessary, which is most times.
4. When you have heard both sides of the situation, start to look flexibly at possibilities to arrive at a satisfactory solution.

FEELINGS

Feelings run high in many customer service situations, yet often these go unacknowledged. An assertive approach acknowledges the feelings present, particularly when the progress of the conversation is slow or circular, taking a long time to get nowhere. Acknowledging feelings often has the effect of unblocking the situation.

For example, you may find yourself getting angry, tense or pressured in dealing with a customer. The customer may be getting more and more irritated. By acknowledging these feelings you bring a sense of reality and

Acknowledging feelings – both your own and the other person's – can unblock a tense situation.

openness to a situation which can lower the temperature and put a more rational frame on the conversation. You might say 'You're obviously irritated that you've been passed through to a second person to deal with your problem. For my part, I'm sorry you've been put in this position but I'm having difficulty piecing together the facts'.

MATCHING WHAT YOU SAY WITH THE WAY YOU SAY IT

In face-to-face situations many people let themselves down by failing to mirror the words they are saying with their:
- voice, its pitch, pace and speed
- posture
- facial expression and eye contact.

Study your body language and make sure it is not at odds with what you are trying to convey.

This can mean at worst that the speaker comes across as insincere or ambiguous. They have diluted their message and the customer may be left wondering about them. Were they really sorry? Did they really mean it was a pleasure to serve them? With a colleague, try saying 'It was a pleasure to serve you' in as many different voices and expressions as you can think of. Notice the different effects they have.

How does an assertive person behave? Think about the following:
- Voice – pleasantly friendly but firm and evenly paced
- Posture upright but not rigid
- Alert but friendly face and plenty of eye contact
- Open manner.

An unassertive person may have:
- Taut, high pitched voice
- Rigid posture
- Tense or hostile expression with poor eye contact
- Folded arms or crossed legs
- Fidgeting mannerisms.

COPING WITH DIFFERENT SITUATIONS

Let us look at a variety of situations and see how an assertive response can be achieved.

Coping with aggression

Aggressive customers are always difficult to deal with. An assertive approach allows customers to express their feelings, to calm down. They will only do this when they are given full rein to say what they feel and why. This means listening and summarising what they have said then stating your position simply and clearly.

Saying 'no'
No one likes to say 'no' in dealing with customers but there are times when that has to be said. Remember, when saying no:
1. Decline with a reason
2. Do not apologise profusely or excessively
3. Make sure you have all the information – clarify if necessary.

Being positive
Negative situations ('We can't do this because . . .') can be made worse by a negative approach. Being assertive contributes to creating a positive impression. To be positive:
1. Do not hide behind other people ('It's company policy', 'It was the computer', 'They should have told you').
2. Do not beat about the bush – be direct.
3. Put over positively what you *can* do. Do not ramble on with lots of excuses about what you *cannot* do.

Meetings
It is often important to be assertive at meetings – to get your voice heard, but in the right way. The following points will help.
1. Pick your moment to say what you have got to say – too soon and no one will listen, too late and minds have been made up and people have moved on. A good method of starting is to pick out something you can agree with in what has just been said.
2. Make sure you understand what other people are saying. Do not get so involved in your own thoughts you do not hear.
3. Do not allow yourself to be too readily interrupted or diverted until you have made your point.
4. Check the reaction you are getting from others to your points.

SUMMARY

Assertiveness is about respecting yourself as well as the customer. An aggressive approach fails to respect the customer. A passive approach leads to timidity and guilt, with the consequent poor communication to the customer. In order to treat customers in an assertive manner:
- Know what you want or need to do
- Listen to the customer, learn as much as you can about their point of view
- State your position clearly and directly

- Work towards a position where the customer feels understood and respected and that at least some of their needs have been met.

If you wish to be more assertive

1. Identify six situations where you would like to change your behaviour. Start with the easiest and work out a script of what you will say and do. Rehearse these words with yourself in front of a mirror or with a colleague or someone outside work.
2. Practise assertiveness in conjunction with listening especially carefully to what the customer or other person is saying, trying not to judge them too quickly. Summarise what you have heard. Put yourself in their shoes. What are their priorities and objectives?
3. Try replaying situations where you have come off badly. Learn from your mistakes. Imagine yourself as confident, assertive and successful in that interaction. What do you say in such a situation? How would the other person react and how would the outcome be different? By doing this you stand a better chance of being successful. In preparation for a new situation, again visualise the successful you.
4. Coach your staff to be assertive with customers, and to know the distinction between assertive, aggressive and passive behaviour. Consider setting up some off-the-job training to rehearse assertive behaviour in familiar customer scenarios.

How do you reply?

To practise increasing your assertiveness try writing down an assertive response to these customer situations:

1. Why does this company never do things properly?
   Your reply

2. It's no better than I would have expected from you.
   Your reply

3. I've spent three weeks trying to get an answer! I'm extremely angry with you.
   Your reply

4. Give me an answer or I'm going straight to the top.
   Your reply

5. That's a crazy answer you've just given me.
   Your reply

6. Well, don't you worry about my company going out of business because of you.
    Your reply

7. I'll never get a straight answer from you.
    Your reply

8. Come off it! You must think I was born yesterday.
    Your reply

9. Are you really sure that's the correct way to do it?
    Your reply

Check your answer against these suggestions.
1. Why does this company never do things properly?
    Your reply
    I'm sorry to hear that. You sound very frustrated. I believe we've got a good track record of doing things well. How can we resolve this now?
2. It's no better than I would have expected from you.
    Your reply
    I can see you're disappointed by what's happened. That makes me feel bad because I've worked hard to try and meet your needs. How can we improve on this?
3. I've spent three weeks trying to get an answer! I'm extremely angry with you.
    Your reply
    I can understand your anger. Three weeks is a long time to wait. I'd like to resolve this quickly now. Would a loan copy help you?
4. Give me an answer or I'm going straight to the top.
    Your reply
    I appreciate how urgent this is. My managing director would be happy to speak to you, but I've got the information you need here.
5. That's a crazy answer you've just given me.
    Your reply
    You're obviously surprised by my answer. Let me explain in more detail.
6. Well don't you worry about my company going out of business because of you.
    Your reply
    I recognise this is a serious problem for you and I'm worried that you feel like this. Let me explain exactly what I've done so far and then let's talk about what we need to do next.
7. I'll never get a straight answer from you.

34 MANAGING THE CUSTOMER INTERFACE

Your reply
You feel I'm not giving you reliable information? That makes me feel disappointed. I want to keep your business and for you to trust us. The goods will be with you by Wednesday.

8. Come off it! You must think I was born yesterday.

Your reply
You sound annoyed and as if you think I'm fobbing you off. Let me explain the details of the agreement more fully.

9. Are you really sure that's the correct way to do it?

Your reply
You sound doubtful about the method I'm suggesting. This is the recommended route based on our experience. What particular aspect are you concerned about?

◀ CHAPTER 4 ▶

MANAGING THE PROBLEM-SOLVING PROCESS

There are three important aspects of problem solving considered in this chapter:
1. How you encourage individuals and teams to solve problems quickly and successfully
2. What methods are available to identify and solve problems
3. How you organise to ensure effective management of the problem-solving process for a fast and responsive customer service.

Success is based on getting right all three of these interlocking components of the problem-solving process.

INDICATORS OF INEFFECTIVE PROBLEM SOLVING

Do you and your team suffer from any of these?
- Low motivation and morale
- People easily getting beaten by problems
- Poor training and knowledge
- No one getting positive feedback from success. Plenty of criticism
- No one owning problems. They get bounced between departments
- Other departments constantly criticising you
- Information hard to obtain
- Mistakes of any sort being jumped on vigorously with no one spared public criticism
- Managers passing the buck and not backing their staff
- Poor means of measuring and rewarding performance
- Unrealistic timescales

- Pressure from overwork
- Unsystematic approach
- Poor leadership and coordination.
- No clearly recognised means of planning ahead or prioritising urgent or important items.

If you have ticked several of these points you should explore opportunities to improve your problem-handling capability. This chapter makes some suggestions to help you do this.

ENCOURAGING PEOPLE

Managers should set up a positive climate for problem handling. People must have the correct mind-set to solve problems, particularly the more complex or unusual ones, and to spot something different about an apparently routine situation.

It is helpful to log the problems you receive from customers and to analyse their causes and frequency. In this way you will learn which are the most critical problems. However, this will only represent the tip of the iceberg since few people take the trouble to complain.

To create the right climate for problem solving, regularly review and give feedback to individuals in your team on problem-handling progress, as follows.

- Praise success and point out shortcomings. This works well if done sincerely and specifically. On the other hand if there is a problem that needs correcting, act quickly while the matter is fresh in the individual's mind.
- Ensure knowledge and skills are up to date and adequate.
- Provide frequent information updates to give staff confidence that they have the latest position to give to the customer.
- Give sufficient authority to staff to sort out the bulk of the problems. Do this by analysing the most likely complaints and delegating authority so that staff can decide without referring upwards, for example cash refunds up to a certain limit.
- Consider means to check morale. With larger departments, attitude surveys using anonymous questionnaires can be very revealing for the manager, by providing insights into areas of team concern. Typical questions gauge employees' knowledge of the direction and objectives of the organisation, their opinions on how they are managed, their training and development, communication and teamwork. It is also possible to address issues such as pay and conditions and working environment as part of attitude surveys.

In addition to surveys, informally 'walking the job' will also give you

useful clues and help you to notice any potential 'downspots'. Make sure you set aside time regularly to be seen around and get to know people and the problems they face.
- Seek out ways to keep up morale. Special events like quarterly business reviews could help, plus news bulletins and incentive prizes.
- Encourage staff to adopt a customer problem. Do not let them get into the habit of forgetting a problem once it has been passed to another department. Set up a procedure to log and chase customer issues through to their completion.
- Be an active representative and carrier of information for your department within the company and with customers. Internally maintain and encourage positive relationships with other departments. Poor working relationships internally can sap energy and morale. Be a go-between to channel feedback back to your department from the customer and to provide information and positive news to the customer.
- Set achievable timescales and balance workload so that staff do not feel they are constantly running to stand still.
- With some problems it is helpful to encourage task groups to address the issues. Promote a free-thinking and constructive environment. Do this by praising new ideas and wide-ranging thinking which does not narrow down the options too soon.
- Introduce a staff service quality improvement team to promote improved methods of working. (See Chapter 6 on total quality management for more detail.)
- Ensure your management information system captures both hard and soft data to keep you fully up to date on customer needs and concerns.
- See problems and complaints as opportunities to explore ways to give a better service and demonstrate to the customer your power to recover a situation and build loyalty.

A SYSTEMATIC APPROACH TO PROBLEM SOLVING

A problem can be efficiently tackled using a step-by-step approach as a framework. This has the benefit of consistency. What often happens is that people tackle problems in different ways and the result is a muddle or that people jump to conclusions too quickly and waste time going up blind alleys. Consider the following questions:

Most problems can be efficiently tackled using a systematic step-by-step approach.

- What is the situation?
- What is the problem (or problems)? Which is the most important one?
- What do we need to do to tackle the problem? What information do we need?
- What ideas have we got for solutions?

- How do we implement the solution?
- What can we learn from the process?

This process is not always in a sequence: you may need to return to previous stages as you get more information. At regular stages, as well as at the end, reviews are useful for checking whether things are going in the right direction. Reviews are often neglected in the rush to get a problem solved and as a result useful lessons are not learnt.

METHODS FOR IDENTIFYING AND SOLVING PROBLEMS

Here are some practical suggestions for identifying and solving problems.

Fact gathering

Get the facts. It is too easy to jump to the wrong conclusions because of poor fact gathering. Ensure your staff follow a procedure of careful questioning and listening. Here is a step-by-step procedure for getting the facts:
1. Ask open questions (who, what, where, when, why?)
2. Listen carefully and summarise key points
3. Use follow-up questions to clarify and to get to the detail
4. Agree what actions you will take.

Many problems need careful analysis and a rigorous approach. Ensure your systems help this to happen. Panics and crises as a matter of course will almost certainly impact on the quality of your solutions.

Planning ahead and using charts

Encourage planning ahead to anticipate problems. Where appropriate use formal techniques like critical path analysis, perhaps using paper or a whiteboard. One approach to charting problems is the fishbone method, illustrated in Figure 4.1. Start with the central problem as the 'backbone' and then put all causes of the issue as bones from this backbone. You can then tack additional causes in turn on to each bone until the problem is fully analysed.

Use this rule to prioritise the order in which the causes should be tackled: what will give the most return for the effort expended?

Creative problem solving

Sometimes it can help to use creative problem solving skills, where you let your mind roam freely so as to gain a fresh outlook. Creativity needs a relaxed unconstrained environment, so special management is needed in most hectic customer service environments to make sure you have favourable conditions in which to be creative.

MANAGING THE PROBLEM-SOLVING PROCESS 39

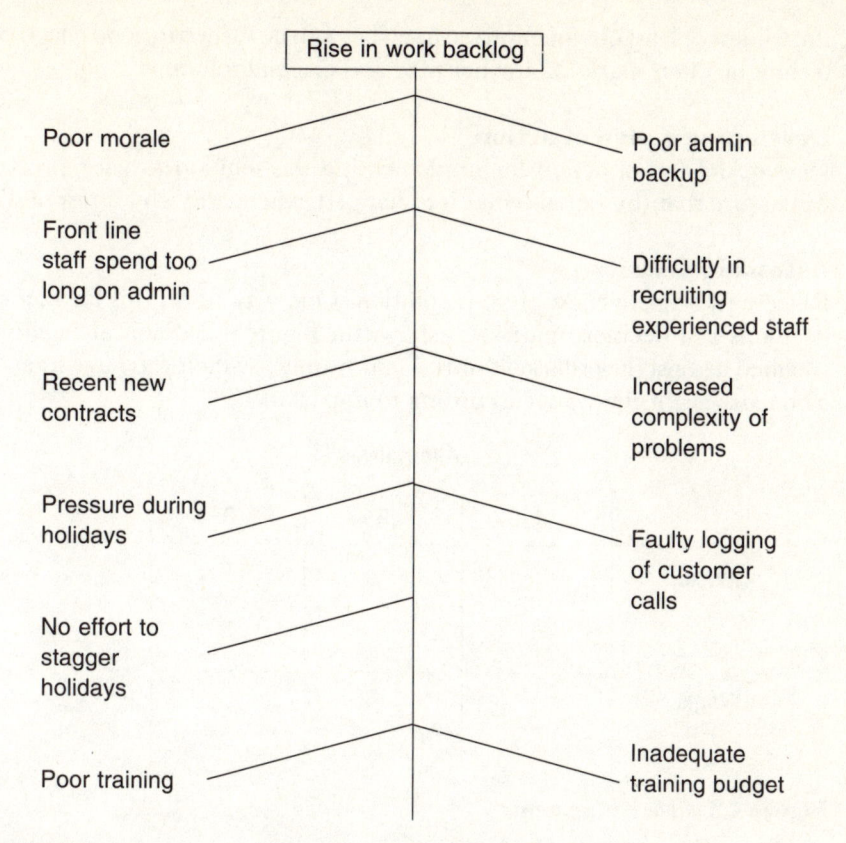

```
                    ┌─────────────────────┐
                    │ Rise in work backlog │
                    └─────────────────────┘

  Poor morale ──────╲                    ╱────── Poor admin
                                                 backup

  Front line
  staff spend too ──╲                    ╱────── Difficulty in
  long on admin                                  recruiting
                                                 experienced staff

  Recent new ───────╲                    ╱────── Increased
  contracts                                      complexity of
                                                 problems

  Pressure during ──╲                    ╱────── Faulty logging
  holidays                                       of customer
                                                 calls

  No effort to
  stagger ──────────╲                    
  holidays

                                                 Inadequate
  Poor training ────╲                    ╱────── training budget
```

Figure 4.1 *Example of a partly completed fishbone diagram*

Brainstorming

Brainstorming is one technique which can be useful in creative problem solving.

In a group all ideas are written down on a flip chart or whiteboard as quickly as they can be shouted out. Do not evaluate at this stage. 'Write it down before you knock it down' is good advice here. Then start to sift out the ideas using more critical analytical methods.

The same process can be done on your own to map out many possibilities or ideas, however tentative or wild they seem at first. They may have the germ of a sound solution.

Brainstorming is a tried and tested technique for creative problem solving and finding novel solutions.

Evaluating suggestions

When you have generated ideas for possible solutions to your problem, you need to evaluate each idea properly to see its pros and cons rather than jumping to the obvious conclusion. Concentrate on those ideas which seem the wildest or least obvious and see how they can be turned to good effect. This technique often sparks off further new and original solutions.

Developing a plan of action
Develop a plan of action for implementing the solution to your problem. Make sure that this details what is to happen, when, and who is responsible.

Assessing decisions
Review the effectiveness of your solution. One way to do this for complex decisions is a decision matrix, as shown in Figure 4.2. Each alternative is weighed against the criteria – 'musts' and 'wants' – which you have spelt out. You can weight the wants according to importance.

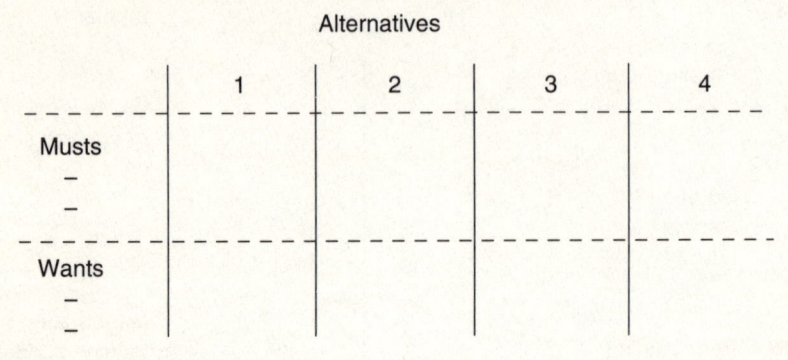

Figure 4.2   *The decision matrix*

Project management
When introducing substantial change, you may need to set up a project team. Carefully and systematically plan each stage and avoid the temptation to get started before you are ready. At the beginning, objectives should be clarified and agreed. At the middle, implementation and corrective action is applied. Then, at the end, the final output is delivered and reviewed. Cost and resource monitoring and control are vital to keep the project well managed despite the inevitable changes.

SUMMARY

- Set a positive climate for handling problems with your team which allows for an appropriate mix of logical processes and free thinking.
- Let everyone have their say. Do not be too hard on people who make the occasional mistake, otherwise people will cover up.

- Adopt a structured problem-solving technique to help identify problems and generate possible solutions. This will help to avoid fruitlessly wasting resources in pursuit of the wrong problem or the wrong solution.
- Encourage a spirit of creativity within your department. This will not just happen of its own accord. Allow your people to get away from business distractions and use a technique such as brainstorming to open minds.

EXERCISES

1. Analyse the most recent important problem which your department dealt with. How did you deal with the situation? Consider what factors affected the situation; for example:
    - What pressures were there?
    - How much information did you have?

    What should you do differently next time?
2. Utilise some of the creative problem-solving techniques next time you tackle a difficult problem. Encourage your staff to think creatively of possible solutions to the problem. Consider introducing training in creative techniques.
3. Review how systematically your staff deal with problems. Assess whether your people would benefit from some training or coaching in systematic problem-solving skills.
4. Review the last occasion on which you were involved in managing a project. How well did you prepare for the project? Were your timescales realistic? Did you successfully coordinate everyone's contribution? How well did you coordinate with the customer? What did you learn from this experience?

◀ **CHAPTER 5** ▶

POSITIVE PERSUASION AND NEGOTIATION

In this chapter we look at:
- How you handle situations where conflict can occur
- How you keep it positive when it all sounds negative
- The components of persuading and influencing
- The art of negotiation: how you succeed.

Any company which serves the customer will recognise that it can no longer just quote the rules to a customer and expect obedience and loyalty. You need to find more flexible and skilful ways of keeping your customers loyal so that they feel that you have done all you can to help their business. That is where the skills of persuasion, selling and influencing come in.

Imagine the following situation. You are a company which supports customers who have bought your computer software. Every software has malfunctions or 'bugs' in it. Some are easy to fix, some are not. The software you sell has a particular bug which cannot be fixed without expensive rework, so it will not be put right until six months' time when the new version will be released. How do you sell this to a customer who wants a solution to the bug now? Do you say:

1. Sorry it's company policy. You'll just have to live with it I'm afraid or go elsewhere.
2. The problem is it's too expensive to fix. You must realise we can't spend too much money correcting problems in an older version. It's just not profitable.
3. I realise your business is suffering because of this. Can we help you work around the problem?
4. The next release will have this corrected and be more useful to you. I'll put your name down for the first release in June.

The answer you give may determine how the customer will feel about continuing to purchase your products.

The problem with the first response is that it is inflexible – it makes no attempt to meet the customer's problem. The second answer is helpful in that it gives an explanation, but again fails to address the customer's concerns. The third answer recognises the concerns of the customer and tries to move forward. The fourth answer tries to sell the benefits of waiting, though it does not deal with the customer's immediate concern.

Each of these, in the right context, might be appropriate. In the rest of this chapter we look at various ways to approach these kinds of situations and to decide how to respond in ways which best meet the customer's needs.

WHEN THE GOING GETS TOUGH

Do you hear your staff saying any of these?
- 'I can't do anything. It's other people who've got to sort it out.'
- 'There are lots of idiots around here. I seem to be the only one who knows what's going on.'
- 'Don't blame me, I'm only passing on the message.'
- 'I'll do anything to shut them up.'
- 'It's your problem not mine.'
- 'The facts speak for themselves.'
- 'I just let it all wash over me.'
- 'I don't know why some customers make such a fuss.'
- 'I really got him then. I made him look really silly.'
- 'It's best to do and say the minimum you can get away with.'

If you hear any of these from your staff, it is time to examine ways to increase their ability to present a helpful persuasive image to the customer and enable them to stay positive.

WHICH STRATEGY DO YOU ADOPT?

In every tricky customer situation you can adopt a certain strategy. Which one most closely resembles your typical stance? Can you see these types in your staff?

The shark
This person uses their position to force their point of view and does not give much ground or listen too carefully to the customer's point of view. In a less overtly aggressive way this approach can take the form of quoting company policy and sticking to a set of rules or saying that the facts speak for themselves, ignoring other interpretations or information. It is almost as if they are saying: 'I'm right and if you don't like it that's your problem.'

Staying on top is what counts here. It puts the customer into the losing position, while the shark wins. But the shark only wins in the short term, since this approach builds up bad feeling and encourages customers to look elsewhere where they are treated with more respect.

The teddy bear
The teddy bear wants to be everybody's friend. So he or she will go to great lengths to avoid conflict. He or she will quickly and readily agree with the customer, even if this means putting the company in a poor light. While teddy bears are fine when things go well and everyone is happy smiles, they will go through agonies if they have to refuse a customer or give bad news.

The turtle
This type turns and scurries off quickly. Turtles are so anxious to avoid getting too involved they are quick to pass the buck, or blame others. They come over as indifferent to customers' real needs – all they want is a quiet life. The danger here is that the customer views that person as the company, and that the company will be perceived as unhelpful and unresponsive. This person costs the company dear by apathetic indifference which damages company image and reputation.

The fox
The fox is crafty. Foxes cynically go for the quick fix. If it costs the company long term, that is someone else's problem. It is a very pragmatic stance which stitches together a deal for the moment; it gets the customer off their back. As a strategy it appears superficially to work quite well, certainly in the short term. In the long term it can have negative consequences. It will often lead to inconsistencies as this person strives to do whatever will solve the immediate situation. It may lead to broken promises.

The customer who deals regularly with this person will feel that they cannot entirely trust them. The fox goes for the line of least resistance every time, to fix the current problem, rather than find the best long-term solution. In dealing with the fox, the customer is likely to be unclear about the principles of the company and feel uncertain about policy and procedures.

The owl
This type of person is wise and through their willingness to confront difficult issues openly, has got the long-term interests of the company at heart. Owls have the ability to turn their heads 360 degrees; they strive to meet customer's needs every time while keeping a clear eye on the company's interests. They will do their best to arrive at a joint solution, where both sides feel they can at least live with a situation and more often than not feel good about it. They know that this will involve tracking and following a problem through the company to a satisfactory solution. It may mean confronting other departments and negotiating internally to get the best for the customer. It will also mean being open about the facts of a situation to the customer and taking full responsibility as the company representative.

The owl values the long-term relationship with the customer and actively seeks to build trust, openness and common understanding. The owl is a customer service winner.

HOW TO BE PERSUASIVE

Persuasion involves exercising skills to bring about a change in the other person's views and perceptions. It is particularly useful in service situations because it builds customer loyalty and satisfaction.

You are much more likely to put you and the company in the best light if you seek to persuade using the following principles.

Be clear where you stand
Too often people go into situations unclear of their objectives and priorities. This soon becomes apparent when the customer makes requests or comments which alter the position.

When negotiating with customers be clear about your own objectives and priorities.

Be prepared to give to get agreement
Making a concession will oil the wheels to agreement. This may only be a small movement. For example, it may be the offer of literature. Whatever it is, the aim is to demonstrate generosity, to see a situation from the customer's point of view and move towards them. You should aim for concessions which are valuable to the customer and cheap for you.

Put yourself in the customer's shoes
There is research evidence to suggest that if customers feel you understand them, that you have a good relationship with them, then they are more likely to be persuaded by you. So ask yourself: What does he or she need to hear? What does he or she want? How does he or she see the situation? Do not be clouded by shutting your mind to what you see as an illogical or 'unreasonable' position on the part of the customer.

Talk benefits not features
It is very easy for you to see the features of a product or service, the technical aspects of what you produce. But you will be far more persuasive if you talk about advantages and benefits to the customer. Below are examples which illustrates the difference.

Put yourself in the customers' shoes and talk about those aspects of a product or service that are important to *them*.

A feature	*A benefit*
This is an AB widget which has three parts	The AB widget has three parts for ease of assembly which you said was important to you.
Our engineers work from home locally	Engineers are never more than one hour away from you and you get your problem fixed quickly, which you said is a priority.

A benefit is more persuasive because it helps customers to see something from their perspective.

If you cannot see the benefit of a particular feature, a useful technique is to keep asking yourself 'so?' until you get to it. For example:

We have a 24 hour helpline.
So?
You can phone in any time day or night.
So?
You can get immediate help with your problem.
Etc.

Talk person to person

Talk the language the customer will understand, in their terms not yours. Because you are dealing with your product or service all the time, you will be tempted to take your jargon for granted in a way that might baffle the customer.

Think before you speak

If you are initiating the contact, do not speak to the customer until you have the facts at your fingertips and you have thought through your position. If you need time to get the facts, say to the customer you will call back when you have got the data and collected your thoughts.

Listen to the replies and act on them

Good listening involves concentrating on what the customer is saying, sometimes for long periods. It involves asking questions about what you have heard and grasping what is really meant. It means being flexible about how to solve a situation in the light of what you are hearing.

THE POWER OF THE POSITIVE APPROACH

You can help generate a positive climate by using positive words. Do not talk yourself and your company down.

Negative approach	*Positive approach*
It isn't available yet	It will be available in a month
The service contract is expensive	The contract offers a high-quality service
She's out today	How can I help?
You'll have to pay £60 extra for the extended warranty	For £60 you can have cover for two years

POSITIVE PERSUASION AND NEGOTIATION 47

Persuasion will not always achieve the resolution of a difficulty. You may need another key skill to move things along to a resolution, the skill of negotiation.

NEGOTIATING

It is not always recognised that we all negotiate in customer service situations. This involves situations where the parties start off from different perspectives but want to reach agreement. However, willingness to negotiate is just the start of the negotiation process. It takes a good deal of skill to negotiate successfully. Since skilful negotiation is such a useful asset in customer service, we will examine the key components of it.

Any negotiation goes through stages. Awareness of these stages will help you to determine what skills and approaches you need to adopt at a particular point in a negotiation.

1. *Preparation.* This includes setting targets, usually as a range from the ideal through to your resistance points, from where you should not move. Preparation also involves prior thinking about the other party's concerns and interests. Managers need to take preparation seriously and not just 'play it by ear'.
2. *Preliminaries.* This early discussion involves finding out:
   - Where you both stand
   - What is important to you both?
   - The areas of agreement and disagreement?
   - How big the gap between you is.
3. *Movement.* This usually takes place in small steps after a tentative toe in the water. After suggestions of possible options or ways forward, one or both parties will start to concede and move towards each other. In customer situations, it will be up to you to make progress by making proposals to bring about movement.
4. *Agreement.* The flow may not be smoothly step by step, but the conclusion of a negotiation should leave both parties feeling satisfied and clear about what has been agreed. It is your responsibility to ensure both of you know the basis for the agreement.

Winners and losers

Imagine you are negotiating with a customer over the price of a big service contract. The customer has put forward the argument that for a contract of this importance they should receive a discount of 10 per cent. You feel that this is more than you can afford but equally you do not wish to lose the customer's business.

In customer situations you need to aim for both sides feeling happy with the outcome – a *win/win* situation. No other option is satisfactory in the long run.

Aim for a win/win conclusion – where both parties feel satisfied, even if they haven't come out with everything they originally wanted.

In this situation you may suggest that they can have the discount if they are prepared to pay the money up front instead of the normal staged payments. After discussion they agree to this. To them the 10 per cent is vital. You feel you have kept the customer's goodwill for only a small true cost to your business.

As shown in Figure 5.1, there are four options in total. Here are the other three:

Lose/win.
1. If in the situation described above you finally agree to the discount the customer is requesting you may feel you have made too many concessions. You may well feel you want to load the price in future contracts. You may dread justifying the deal to senior management and feel that you have been pushed into a corner. When you deal with this customer in future you may feel resentful and unwilling to give ground so readily in negotiations. In this instance you will have a lose/win situation: you lose, the customer wins.

Win/lose.
2. If you stick to the original price and do not agree to the discount the customer may eventually reluctantly agree to your terms. You may feel good about the deal, but the customer walks away unhappy, perhaps determined to 'get even' in the future. It will have undermined long-term relationships perhaps to the point where the customer seeks out your competitors. This will be win/lose.

Lose/lose.
3. The worst of all worlds is that neither party is happy. You do not agree to the discount and the customer decides not to make the purchase. This is a lose/lose situation. Both feel that the other is being unreasonable. For your part you have lost a customer who may well not come back. The customer may have forgotten all the goodwill you have built up.

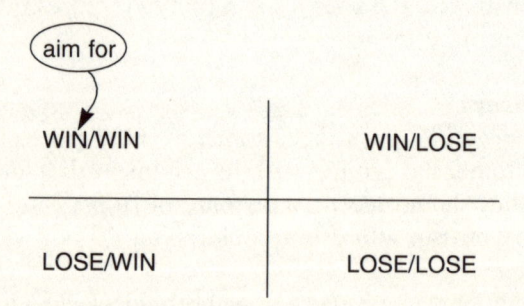

(aim for) ↓ WIN/WIN	WIN/LOSE
LOSE/WIN	LOSE/LOSE

Figure 5.1 *Winners and losers*

To arrive at a win/win solution you should take time to determine each other's objectives – what is important to you and the customer. Then you can apply the principles of give and take from some commonly understood objectives. What options could you put forward in the situation described above? The full discount but a longer contract? What can the customer concede to you? In this instance perhaps a lower discount but a speedier service. Thinking creatively, exploring both parties' objectives and all possible solutions, has led to a satisfactory outcome. In this way both sides arrive at a win/win solution.

TIPS ON NEGOTIATION

Research suggests that experienced and skilled negotiators operate by the following principles.
1. Prepare well, not just in your terms but in terms of how the customer sees the situation. Consider various options and possible concessions. Guard against 'a single way forward' approach both in preparation and during the negotiation. Research has shown this often comes unstuck in the face of the changing needs of a situation.
2. Be explicit about your objectives. This will help both of you to know where you are coming from.
3. Be open about how you feel. Keeping your cards too close to your chest unsettles the other party and leads to excessive caution. Signal your intentions – for example, 'I'd like to raise the issue of x'.
4. Concede slowly in small, not big jumps. If you concede too early or too readily you will give the impression that there is more to come.
5. If in doubt, ask questions. Clarify understanding by asking questions; avoid glossing over issues since this may lead to incorrect expectations or assumptions.
6. Summarise regularly throughout and particularly at the end of a negotiation. It is surprising how misunderstandings can develop which inhibit progress and a satisfactory negotiation. Any lingering lack of clarity should be removed before the negotiation breaks up.
7. Let both sides 'win'. Aim for both sides to come out feeling good about the deal so that it will enhance not damage long-term relationships.
8. Avoid irritating the other person. Phrases that are like a red rag to a bull are: 'it's policy', 'it's fair', 'with respect'. Do not make digs at the other person or veiled critical or sarcastic comments. Look for things you can agree about rather than immediately homing in on the areas of disagreement. In this way you build up solutions by developing common ground rather than destroying it.
9. Do not rise to the bait if the temperature rises. Make sure you avoid responding to aggression with aggression. You will end up in a vicious downhill spiral and get further and further away from agreement. Try not to take the issue too personally if you are attacked.

MANAGING THE CUSTOMER INTERFACE

SUMMARY

- Adopt a positive and flexible approach in dealing with situations where conflict between you and the customer may occur. Aim for a win/win outcome.
- To be persuasive, know your objectives and priorities and carefully consider the customer's point of view. Be prepared to make an effort to reach agreement: a short-term victory may lead to a longer-term worsening of the relationship.
- When negotiating with a customer, prepare your case well. Establish where the customer stands and what are the likely areas of agreement. Be prepared to suggest concessions in the areas where you do not agree. Where possible look for something in return for a concession. Try to look for concessions which are cheap for you and valuable to the customer.

EXERCISES

1. Think about the last time you needed to influence someone about something important to you. How successful were you? What factors affected the outcome? How did you feel? Consider other possible strategies and behaviours which might have been more successful. How can you apply this to the next issue you need to deal with?
2. Sharpen up your analytical tools by consciously observing the persuasive and influencing styles other people are using. Notice the effect they have.
3. Set yourself improvement targets. Pick one area at a time and work at it. Make the targets specific; for example, I will ensure I write out my objectives for the three user group meetings I will attend in the next month.
4. Ask a colleague to sit down with you when you are negotiating with customers and give you some feedback on how you are doing.

◀ CHAPTER 6 ▶

TOTAL QUALITY MANAGEMENT

This chapter considers these questions:
- What steps you can take to ensure a total quality approach in all your dealings with the customer
- What customer-friendly procedures are
- How you ensure that you are meeting the requirements of your customers.

TOTAL QUALITY MANAGEMENT

Quality and customer satisfaction must be paramount for everyone in service-orientated organisations. Many managers feel that, at the end of the day, achieving customer satisfaction is down to one thing. It might be:
- Getting a customer-orientated attitude
- Involving the whole company, not just front line staff
- Keeping track of complaints
- Streamlined systems
- Quality awareness
- Close relationship with suppliers
- Teamwork
- Thorough training
- Having the right product
- Empowerment and involvement at all levels
- Appropriate incentives and awards
- Striving for improvements all the time
- Careful measurements and standards.

One approach applies many of the elements from all these in the pursuit of meeting customers' needs on a continuous basis. It is called 'total quality management' (TQM).

The TQM approach allows an organisation to make a critical assessment of the product and services of the organisation in terms of:
- The processes it adopts to produce them
- The people involved.

Everything the company does is put 'totally' under scrutiny and made subject to continuous quality management and improvement, hence the term total quality management.

People and processes are aligned to the requirements of the customer.

Adopting this approach means that internal customers who provide a service to other parts of the organisation are as important as external customers because they are each part of the quality chain, linking to serve the customer.

WHO BENEFITS BY THIS APPROACH?

1. Primarily the customers: they get what they expect on a continuous basis – right first time, every time.
2. Suppliers: they are clearer what is expected of them, as the people who specify products and services have their organisation's customer needs firmly in mind.
3. Everyone in the company. The adoption of the principles of TQM creates a need for greater involvement, empowerment and participation of employees throughout the organisation in the improvement process. This will often lead to greater job satisfaction as well as improved performance. This is often achieved through an active policy of continuous improvement through service quality improvement teams. Well trained, these employee groups solve problems from first hand experience.

THE PRINCIPLES OF TQM

There are four principles adopted by organisations which practise total quality management (TQM):

1. *Definition of customer requirements*. Defining their customers' requirements so that these needs can be met exactly as the customer wishes, first and every time.

Prevention, not correction, is fundamental to total quality management.

2. *Prevention not correction*. Operating a system to prevent products or services reaching customers which do not conform to their requirements, rather than correcting problems at the finished product or delivery stage.
3. *Performance standards and zero defects*. Setting performance standards which

TOTAL QUALITY MANAGEMENT 53

specify and ensure that there are no defects in the products or services reaching the customer.
4. *Measurement*. Measuring the cost of the defects which occur in the products and services reaching the customer and identifying areas for improvement. Measuring target performance against actual.

SOME TQM QUESTIONS AND ANSWERS

Isn't TQM for manufacturing companies, not service organisations?
TQM started in manufacturing where you can put precise measures on specifications, reliability and product defects. It is now widespread in service organisations.

Isn't it a Japanese import? Britain is very different
Its main application was originally in Japan, but it has been successfully modified to be widely introduced in Britain, Europe and America.

Surely quality is for specialists to look after?
The traditional approach left final quality to specialists – inspectors, engineers and the like. The TQM approach puts the onus on everyone to look out for quality, suggest improvements and keep standards high. Everyone gets involved in looking out for quality improvements.

Quality means the 'goodness' of a product. How can this link back to the customer?
TQM defines quality, not in absolutes but through the eyes of the customer: fitness for purpose or use. This means in effect the *customer* defines the standards, not the service provider.

Isn't TQM about achieving a certificate, such as a British Standard BS5750?
Companies who operate TQM programmes often apply for a British Standards Kitemark BS5750 or the International Standard ISO 9000. This testifies to all concerned that the products and services conform to a recognised standard. But these benchmarks of quality are not an end in themselves.

Isn't TQM an expensive and complicated one-off exercise involving consultants?
No. TQM can be introduced solely by managers and their people. There are techniques involved, but commitment is just as important. Energy comes free! It certainly is not a one-off action. It is a process which goes on forever through systematically identifying improvements.

Isn't TQM just for big organisations?
No. The same principles apply whatever the size and structure of the organisation.

Isn't it all procedure manuals and bureaucracy?
TQM is about being systematic and focused on the customer. If the organisation gets bogged down in rule books it is unlikely to be customer focused.

ARE YOUR PROCEDURES GETTING IN THE WAY OF THE CUSTOMER?

Keep procedures up to date and simple.

Policies, rules and procedures seem to multiply quicker than any virus. If you are not continually vigilant you may well find that you have a complex tangle of procedures which are a struggle for people in the company to follow and make little sense to the bewildered customer. The effect of this is that your organisation becomes hard to do business with. If that is so, you are prey to competitors offering a more streamlined approach which proves more attractive. So, despite a high-quality product or service, you may lose business because the customer is unwilling to waste time and effort to gain access to it.

Here are some signs that your procedures need a fresh look since they are past their useful life:
- Customers start taking their business to competitors. They complain that you take too long, they need to know jargon; they get exasperated at times in dealing with you.
- New customers frequently express surprise or puzzlement in dealing with you. They ask if you can give them a copy of your jargon, your rules.
- New employees take a long time to understand and work to all your procedures.
- Few in your team can readily explain why the procedures are set up in a certain way. They say management is out of touch.
- Your procedure manual is getting bigger and bigger!

WHAT ARE CUSTOMER-FRIENDLY PROCEDURES?

These features typify a customer-friendly system and procedures:
- Customers feel procedures make sense and achieve their objective.
- The words used and the way of doing things do not feel cumbersome or awkward.
- Customers have a positive reaction after dealing with your organisation and feel that you are being courteous, friendly and helpful towards them.
- For the customer, rules do not seem to 'get in the way'. These always seem to be a means to satisfy the customer, or at least to provide a clear explanation where it is not possible to meet needs fully.

HOW TO AUDIT AND REVIEW YOUR PROCEDURES

1. Gather your team together and examine which procedures cause most problems for customers. Ask them to describe clearly the benefits to the customer of working in this way, as though they were talking to a customer. If they cannot do it readily, it is time to review the procedure.

TOTAL QUALITY MANAGEMENT

2. Select some of the procedures and draw a simple flow chart to follow them through the organisation, as though you were the customer dealing with your organisation. Better still, identify real recent customer situations from start to finish. Identify timescales and bottlenecks. Discuss in your team what makes a good impression, what makes a bad impression, how you can improve. Figure 6.1 is an example.

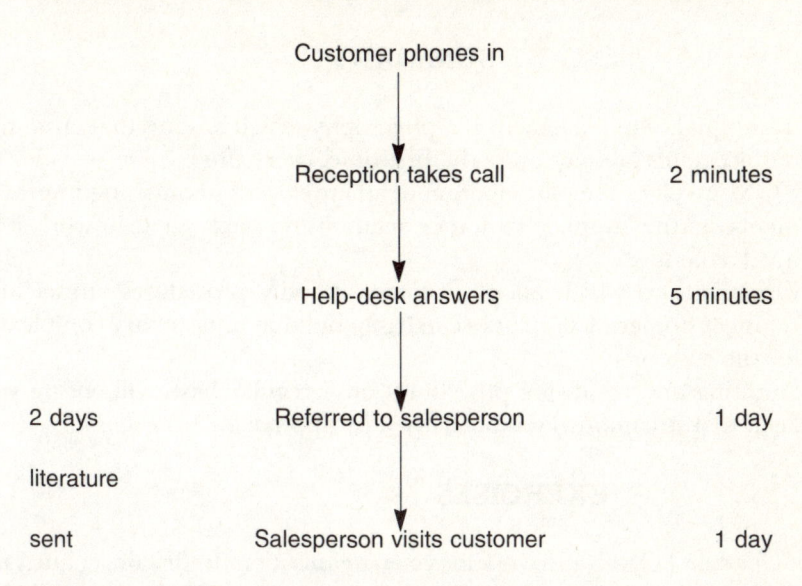

```
                    Customer phones in
                            |
                            v
                    Reception takes call         2 minutes
                            |
                            v
                    Help-desk answers            5 minutes
                            |
                            v
2 days              Referred to salesperson      1 day
literature                  |
sent                        v
                    Salesperson visits customer  1 day
```

Figure 6.1 *Sample flow chart for reviewing a procedure*

TIPS FOR GREATER CUSTOMER FRIENDLINESS

- Keep rules simple. If there are too many or they are too complex, they will be ignored or bypassed.
- Check that working practices and written procedures have not got out of step as actual practices have changed.
- Do not over-standardise. Give defined appropriate discretion for your staff to vary procedures to treat people personally and solve particular problems. But maintain consistency of treatment on essentials.
- Have rapid flexible ways of dealing with mistakes and complaints. Be generous in putting things right.
- Regularly inculcate the principles and values behind your policies and procedures. This ensures understanding and commitment to the spirit of them when procedures are applied.
- Periodically ask customers to describe their experience in dealing with your organisation, based on particular examples.

- Encourage staff through your procedures to 'own' a problem from start to finish, to follow through to ensure a problem gets solved even when they have passed it on to another department. This ensures that demarcation lines do not emerge which act as a barrier to the resolution of difficulties.
- Review how the customer sees the written aspects of your procedures through letters, contracts, orders. Do they match the standards you are trying to create?

SUMMARY

- Total quality management is a philosophy which ensures that customer requirements are met properly, first time, every time.
- TQM involves the participation of all employees in on-going improvements in the supplier/customer relationship through teamwork and involvement.
- Organisations which adopt customer friendly procedures attract and retain customers. Companies can easily build in unnecessary complexity for the customer.
- Auditing and reviewing procedures on a regular basis will ensure you keep to a streamlined customer-friendly approach.

EXERCISES

1. Find out more about whether TQM could work for your organisation. In Britain, contact the Department of Trade and Industry for further information on how TQM can be applied in your business.
2. Map out the customer/supplier relationships that exist within your team or organisation, involving both external and internal customers. Do this as a team and discuss how effective you are in delivering to your customers.
3. Improve the process of dialogue between each customer and you as a supplier to check you have identified all your customer's current requirements. Encourage your team to identify ways to improve their products or services.
4. Ask your customers to help you identify the procedures which cause most problems to them and look at ways of improving these.
5. Set up and train a quality or service improvement team, either with your group or throughout your organisation. It may be useful to pilot a scheme first to iron out the difficulties and use it as an internal reference point for future progress.

◀ CHAPTER 7 ▶

DEALING WITH DIFFICULT CUSTOMER SITUATIONS

In this chapter we consider:
- Your reaction in difficult customer situations
- How you should deal with such situations
- The pitfalls to avoid
- Whether the customer is always right.

In busy service environments, not all customers are easy to please. Some may be pressured for time, others may be particularly demanding. You, in turn, may be under pressure through lack of staff, or time constraints, or because of insufficient resources.

HOW DO YOU REACT IN DIFFICULT CUSTOMER SITUATIONS?

How do you deal with customer complaints, giving a customer bad news, having to say no, or dealing with angry customers?

Tick which of these responses are most typical of you when you encounter difficult customer situations.
- I feel myself getting upset, angry, and losing my cool.
- I try and persuade the customer to see things from my point of view.
- I tend to blame other people in the organisation for the problem.
- I adopt a disinterested approach and let other people deal with the situation.
- I deal with the customer to the best of my abilities, then I take my aggravation out on other people around me.
- I have learnt to respond after listening, not by arguing.

58 MANAGING THE CUSTOMER INTERFACE

Dealing with difficult customer situations can be stressful, both for the customer and you.

Keep a record of the difficult situations you find yourself dealing with over the next month.

You will probably find that you handle some situations better than others. List the situations which you feel you handle competently and those where you recognise you need to improve. Adopt the techniques below to deal with specific difficult situations.

HANDLING CUSTOMER COMPLAINTS

Research shows that the majority of customers do not complain, so the complaints you do receive represent only a small number of the potential complaints. A food manufacturer, for example, discovered that it had mistakenly sent 10,000 packages of product with the wrong formulation out into the retail market. This meant that although the product was not harmful to eat, its taste and flavour would be unpleasant. Yet they only received ten consumer complaints. The likelihood of consumers refusing to purchase the product in the future, however, was very high.

Treat complaints as an opportunity to improve your products and services.

Treat complaints as an opportunity, therefore, to discover how to improve your products and services. The 95 per cent of customers who do not complain are very hard to reach. So remember that those customers who do complain give you a unique opportunity to find out more.

WHAT DO CUSTOMERS LOOK FOR WHEN THEY COMPLAIN?

A customer who has taken the trouble to complain to an organisation expects:
1. Someone to listen actively to the complaint, to be sympathetic and to take responsibility for its resolution
2. To deal with one or two people only, not to be passed from person to person or department to department
3. A quick solution.

So, in dealing with customer complaints, bear in mind the following 'dos' and 'don'ts'.

Dos
- Let the customer explain the situation fully. Listen actively without butting in.
- Show your concern about the situation, using phrases such as 'I'm sorry to hear that', 'that sounds very upsetting for you', or similar terms which reflect your empathy towards what the customer is feeling.
- Show that you will take responsibility for the situation and that you are willing to help.
- Question the customer to get the facts. Write these down and summarise them to show the customer you have fully understood the problem.

- Agree a resolution to the complaint with the customer. Say what you can do, not what you cannot.
- Make sure that you do what you have promised. Follow up with customers to make certain they are happy.
- Keep the customer informed.

Don'ts
- Above all do not appear disinterested.
- Do not lose your temper or show your exasperation with the situation to the customer.
- Do not let the customer know this is a common complaint if you have heard the complaint many times before.
- Do not appear inflexible. Saying, 'Well, it's company policy', or, 'We can't do that', will aggravate the customer.
- Do not blame other people. The customer is not interested in your internal politics; he or she needs a solution to their problem now.

TYPICAL ENCOUNTERS

How do you deal with tricky customer situations? Here are some common types of people which could be typical encounters, together with suggestions to improve your effectiveness.

The volcano
Volcanic types seem eager to pick a fight, to latch on to every word you say and explode before your eyes, inflicting as much damage as possible. They will frequently make comments about you personally, no holds barred.

Response
Never meet fire with fire. Keep your cool, let them have their say. Do not try and interrupt with your side of the story. If they do not calm down, find a way to let them cool off – for example, offer to get some more information or call in someone else.

The knowall
This type reckons he or she knows all there is to know on the subject in hand, although it soon becomes transparently obvious they do not.

Response
A few well-chosen questions will help them to see some of the areas they are not aware of. Working through questions in this way will get them to see the problem more fully themselves. When the problem is clearer to them, suggest a solution, rather than tell.

The hesitant foreigner
This type finds communication very difficult, both in explaining their problem and in understanding your offer of help.

Response
Do not feel offended by apparent rudeness. It is probably unfamiliarity with the subtleties of your language. Equally do not start shouting or talking in pidgin English. Offer to put something in writing for the customer to study at their leisure. Check understanding and be particularly careful in the words you choose, avoiding slang or jargon.

The rambler
These types seem to relish the chance to speak to someone. They refuse to get to the point and ramble on and on about irrelevancies.

Response
Summarise what the customer has said and then keep focusing the discussion back on the subject in hand; for example, 'So how does this prevent the service staff from fixing an appointment?'

The clam
Clams seem to avoid giving you much useful information, and you have to work hard to prise what you need out of them.

Response
Ask open questions. Be friendly. Encourage the customer to talk.

DEALING WITH AGGRESSION

Everyone who deals with customers meets occasions when customers, with whom you are dealing, appear aggressive or angry. They may shout or be rude or sarcastic. Since these situations are ones people usually find hardest to deal with, it is worth while spending time on this issue.

In these difficult situations it is useful to remember that you have a choice in what you say and how you react to the customer.

Getting emotional or angry in your turn will not defuse the situation with the customer. The way to deal with aggression is to:

- Remain calm and in control, and eventually the customer will calm down too
- Remind yourself that the customer's anger is directed not at you but the organisation
- Empathise with the customer and show that you are there to help
- Use the 'stuck record' technique to make your point: stick to what you want to say and repeat your message calmly and persistently

If a customer gets angry, remind yourself that the anger is directed at the organisation, not you.

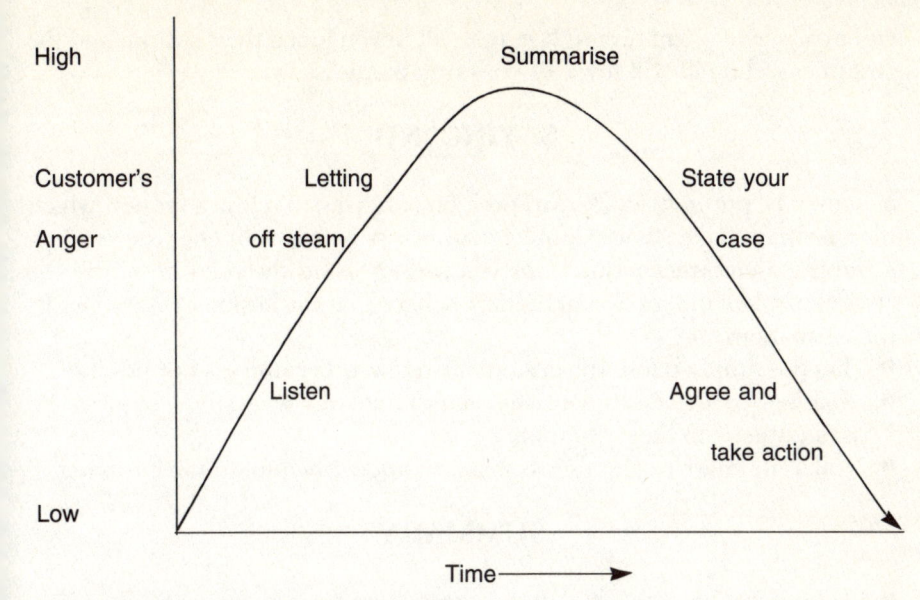

Figure 7.1 *Stages in coping with aggression*

- Act quickly to resolve the customer's concern
- Check back to ensure the customer is happy with what you propose.

GIVING CUSTOMERS BAD NEWS

There may be occasions when you have to tell customers bad news. For example, you may not be able to meet the delivery timescale, you may have lost an important piece of documentation, you may be out of stock of an item. The appropriate action here is:
- Not to beat about the bush. Tell the customer you have bad news. Explain the reasons why. Tell them you are sorry.
- Tell the customer what you *can* do to rectify the situation. Work towards a compromise situation which is agreeable both to you and the customer.
- Make certain you do not make promises you cannot keep. It is better, for example, to be conservative in your time estimates, and to deliver earlier than anticipated, than to be over optimistic and not meet your timescales. This will only disappoint the customer further.

IS THE CUSTOMER ALWAYS RIGHT?

A common saying is that the customer is always right. There may be occasions when you believe that this is not so. However, you need to judge each situation carefully. Telling the customer that they are wrong may cause them

Customers are not always right, but be careful how you tell them this.

embarrassment or confusion. It may result in you losing their custom and the customer feeling ill-will towards your organisation.

SAYING 'NO'

You may be put in the awkward position of having to refuse a request which the customer makes. For example, your company may not offer the product or service a customer requests, or you cannot 'bend the rules' to satisfy the customer's demand, or you genuinely believe that the customer is wrong. In these situations:
- Do not simply refuse the customer's request 'because it's not possible'.
- Explain to the customer why you cannot do what they request. Be sympathetic to their situation.
- Offer alternative solutions so that you appear helpful to the customer.

SUMMARY

- When dealing with difficult customer situations use the skills of:
  - listening and asking questions
  - empathising
  - staying in control through directing your questions and summarising.
- Always show the customer that you are concerned and willing to help. Never express anger, impatience or sarcasm to the customer.
- Act quickly to resolve the situation and make certain that the action is carried through.

EXERCISES

1. Review the last time you had to deal with a difficult customer situation. How well did you control it? What was the outcome? Was the customer left with the impression that you had tried to help?
2. Discuss with your team the procedures you adopt for dealing with complaints. Undertake an analysis of the most common types of complaints. Discuss ways of resolving the causes of these complaints before they reach the customer. Follow up the complaints received over the last six months; ask for feedback.
3. Hold a training session for your team on how to deal with difficult customer situations. Include role play for typical cases.
4. Appoint experienced team members as mentors and coaches to less experienced staff to help them deal more effectively with difficult customer problems and situations. Having someone close at hand to talk the problem through and get advice gives staff the confidence and skill to deal with problem situations.

◀ PART 2 ▶

LEADING YOUR TEAM RESOURCEFULLY

◀ CHAPTER 8 ▶

COMMUNICATION AND GETTING THE MESSAGE ACROSS

This chapter discusses:
- How vital good communication is in providing superior service
- Why it can be difficult to get your message across
- The verbal and non-verbal elements of communication
- The formal mechanisms for improving communication between groups of customers or employees.

As a manager, you are in a web of communication links.

As a manager, you are in a web of communication links. Outside the organisation you need to:
- Contact the all-important customer
- Develop sensitive and accurate means of gathering information from your customers on their changing needs.

Inside the organisation you need to:
- Keep your staff up to date and on track
- Hear from your staff how things are progressing, and any possible problems or barriers to success
- Keep in touch with your manager to keep him or her up to date and to hear what he or she wants and needs
- Keep strong links with other departments to iron out difficulties, gather information and anticipate the way ahead.

Many managers get tangled in the communication web. Since this is such a common part of a manager's task, it is rather disappointing to learn from surveys that the majority of managers are rated poorly on their communication skills by their staff. The end result is that customers find their contacts with a lot of companies unhelpful, slow or inadequate.

Here is a random sample of customers' comments about the service they have received. Do you recognise some of these from your own experience?
- 'She seemed completely disinterested – she just stared blankly at me.'
- 'He was such a nice, helpful person. I would go back there again.'
- 'She seemed to be reading a script. She didn't mean the nice things she was saying.'
- 'He was so rude. He glared at me and made me feel small.'
- 'He really took the trouble to find out what we wanted.'
- 'She even remembered that we had asked for the special if it became available.'

All of these examples involve communication and demonstrate its power in delivering service.

The aim of this chapter is to help you to develop effective communication which:
- Gets the message across clearly and unambiguously
- Creates a positive image with customers
- Makes efficient use of time – yours and the customer's
- Wins business, not loses it.

WHY IS IT SO DIFFICULT TO GET THE MESSAGE ACROSS?

Do any of these sound familiar? Have customers ever said any of these to you or to your staff?
- 'I can't get a word in edgeways.'
- 'I haven't a clue what you're talking about.'
- 'I think we're talking at cross-purposes.'
- 'You don't seem to understand.'
- 'There's no need to take that attitude.'

If these are regular comments, they are sure signs that you need to untangle what is wrong and to adopt a different approach. To find out what can go wrong in communication and why, look at Figure 8.1 and then consider the elements in the communication process. Each element is a variable which will affect the quality of the communication.
- *What you are saying.* This may be very complex. It may be relevant or not. It is no use telling customers about your warehousing system when all they wish to know is the date when their goods will be delivered.
- *The way you are saying it.* The language and tone you use has a critical effect. It needs to be targeted at the customer and their ability to comprehend, and take into account the situation. This also includes, if appropriate, your body language – displaying interest, showing involvement, or, the opposite, showing boredom or inattention.

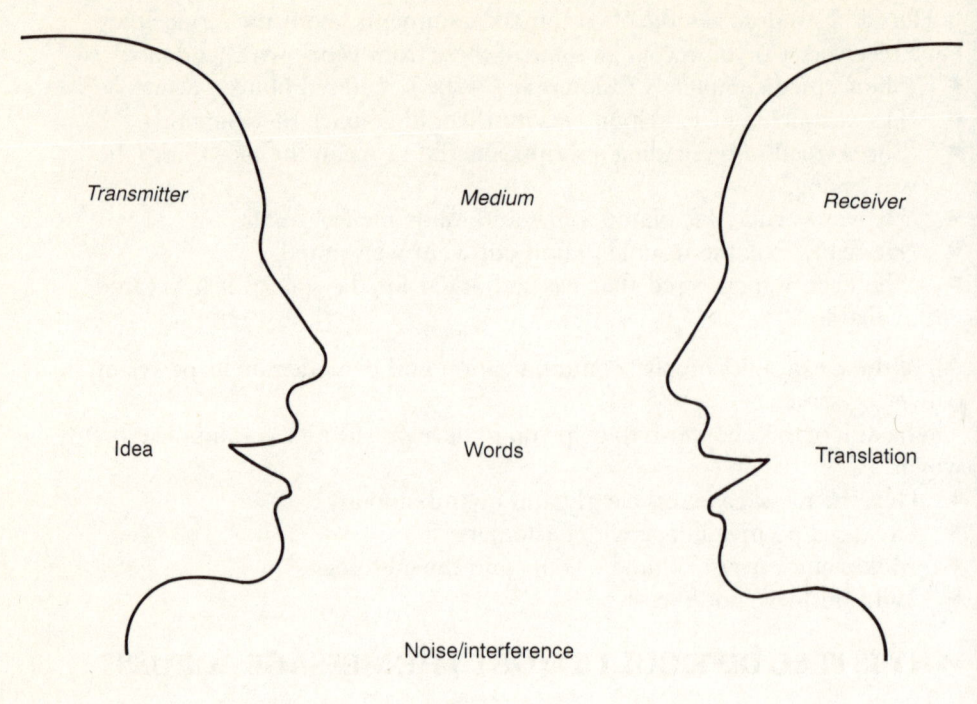

```
Transmitter          Medium              Receiver


   Idea              Words              Translation



              Noise/interference
```

Figure 8.1 *Communication*

- *The medium.* Face-to-face communication is appropriate in some service situations, but not in others. A 'phone call can get access quickly, but you cannot see the other person and how they are reacting – whether they are puzzled, irritated or whatever. Equally, if you send a letter or fax, it gives no opportunity to ask questions, but provides a record and gives the receiver time to consider what to say.

  Choose your communication medium carefully to fit the message. Is it long or short? complex or simple? is there a need for interaction or not?
- *The information giver.* You may or may not be tuned in fully to deliver the message. You may be affected by varying degrees of interest or relevance or how uncomfortable the message makes you feel.
- *The listener.* Communication will be affected by considerations such as: who you are talking to; what their priorities are; how much they know already; their frame of mind.
- *Noise or distracting interference.* Communication will be affected if either party finds it difficult to shut out distractions from other people and the noise around them, such as 'phones in the office. For example, a colleague is trying to catch your eye while you are on the phone to a customer. Or

it might be other claims on your attention which trigger wandering thoughts such as:
- 'It's getting late...'
- 'I must ring...'
* Getting bogged down in irrelevant detail or red herrings.

PREPARATION FOR COMMUNICATION

Figure 8.2 summarises the communication process. With all communication you need to review beforehand:
* *What* you intend to say
* *Who* will receive it
* *Why* you are communicating
* *How* you should choose to get the point over
* *When* you need to do it.

It is particularly important to run through these questions before you communicate a complex message or one which is likely to meet a strong customer reaction. Here is an example of the unintended consequences of communication to a customer.

> This problem has never happened before. On the phone you say: 'Are you sure? This has never happened in three years.' The customer replies angrily: 'I'm not stupid you know.'

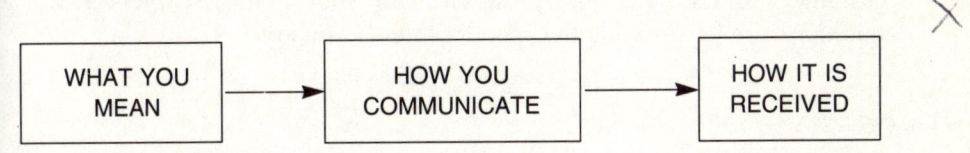

WHAT YOU MEAN → HOW YOU COMMUNICATE → HOW IT IS RECEIVED

Figure 8.2 *The communication process*

TIPS FOR SMOOTH-FLOWING COMMUNICATION

These tips will help you and your staff in communicating with customers. The same principles apply in all your dealings with others.
- Put yourself in the customer's shoes. How is the customer likely to feel in each situation?
- Have relevant information to hand.
- If you are speaking to another person, prepare what you want to say, particularly opening remarks.
- Listen carefully to what is being said.
- Be aware of underlying themes, concerns, feelings.
- Respond to the customers' concerns first and foremost.

- Bring feelings out in the open by briefly describing theirs and, if appropriate, yours.
- Summarise regularly to avoid misunderstandings.
- Agree actions with timescales.

LISTENING

Active listening is an important skill.

Now let us look at listening as a component of communication. Active listening is an important skill which will help you understand customers' needs.

Think of someone you know who is a poor listener. What characteristics do they display? List them down and then compare them with the list below.

Signs of poor listening

Tell-tale signs that someone is not listening are:
- Glazed eyes, fixed expression
- Getting defensive
- Ignoring everything but personal interests
- Interrupting
- Fidgeting, looking away, looking at a watch
- Yawning, looking bored
- Getting distracted by someone's accent, their appearance.

Watch out for these in yourself. Notice and change tack if you see these in customers and do not just press on with your points. Table 8.1 is a questionnaire for assessing how good a listener you are.

Table 8.1 *Listening questionnaire*

Look at each pair of statements and decide which one is true for you. If it is very true, you tick 1 or 5, quite true 2 or 4; 3 is about the middle – neither statement is true.

People say I do not listen enough	1	2	3	4	5	People say I am a good listener
I tend to interrupt customers and finish their sentences	1	2	3	4	5	I let people have their say before I begin to speak
When I am listening I get distracted by things that go on around me	1	2	3	4	5	I successfully make a conscious effort to avoid getting distracted by things around me
I believe in pursuing my ideas forcefully	1	2	3	4	5	I keep an open mind on other people's ideas
When a customer complains I find it hard to see their point of view	1	2	3	4	5	I always try hard to put myself in the customers' shoes

COMMUNICATION AND GETTING THE MESSAGE ACROSS

If my staff ask for time on a personal matter I rarely give them my undivided attention	1	2	3	4	5	I always give my staff my full undivided attention when they ask for personal time
I find I get involved personally with criticism and defend myself	1	2	3	4	5	I step back from most criticism and try to weigh up how much truth there is in it
I find it impossible to listen to people whom I dislike	1	2	3	4	5	I keep listening to what is being said even if I do not like the person
I get impatient when I cannot easily figure out what a customer means because their description is unclear or rambling	1	2	3	4	5	I try to work out what a customer means, even when their description is not clear or rambles
When a customer hesitates, I jump in and fill the silence	1	2	3	4	5	I let the customer finish when he or she hesitates, even if there is silence for a while
I find it difficult to look customers in the eye and to show through my body language that I am interested in what they are saying	1	2	3	4	5	I consciously use open, attentive body language, eg smiling, making eye contact
If I deal with a customer for a long time my mind wanders and I cannot concentrate	1	2	3	4	5	I focus my mind on a particular customer and put other thoughts aside
I believe you can put people into categories, by and large. I am nearly always right when I anticipate how a category will behave	1	2	3	4	5	Although I put a label on some people or groups I am aware of my prejudices and work extra hard to overcome them
I tend to be right about the things I deal with at work. I do not get much value from what other people contribute	1	2	3	4	5	I value other people's contributions and what they have to say
When a customer says something clearly incorrect I put them right straight away	1	2	3	4	5	When a customer says something incorrect I hear them out and ask them questions first before I comment

Scoring

50–75: You listen comparatively well, but do not get complacent!

30–50: There is room for improvement.

less than 30: You should make a serious effort to start listening more fully.

GIVING A CLEAR EXPLANATION

When dealing with customer enquiries face to face or on the 'phone and when answering specific queries, you need to be able to give customers a clear explanation and to make certain that they have understood this. To make sure you answer fully a customer's query:
- Listen actively
- Ask questions to establish their concern
- Decide what you have to say to answer their query
- Use simple and direct language to put your point across
- Explain first the areas the customer will find easiest to understand
- Establish the customer's understanding of the explanation by asking questions
- Check that your explanation answers the customer's query to their satisfaction.

MATCH WHAT YOU SAY BY HOW YOU SAY IT

The message you transmit to customers is conveyed not only by what you say but also by the way in which you say it. Customers can soon tell if the body language you adopt contradicts the verbal message you are giving. The eyes and face are the most obvious areas of the body in which a message is transmitted. If you welcome a customer, for example, yet do not look a person in the eyes, frown or are unsmiling, he or she will soon think you are hostile or cold.

Faces
Look at the simplified pictures of people's faces in Figure 8.3. Draw in the mouth and eyebrows on each face to illustrate the emotions each person is feeling. Notice that the eyes, eyebrows and mouth are clear indications of people's emotions. (The authors' suggestions are given in Figure 8.5 at the end of the chapter.)

Remember to use open gestures if you wish to convey a friendly manner:
- Look the person directly in the eye
- Smile
- Have your arms and legs unclasped.

Figure 8.4 illustrates a friendly versus a hostile stance. Use your own observations of customers and members of staff to see whether the message you are transmitting is well received. Be careful to eliminate barriers to communication with customers and staff such as desks and counters which set you apart from other people.

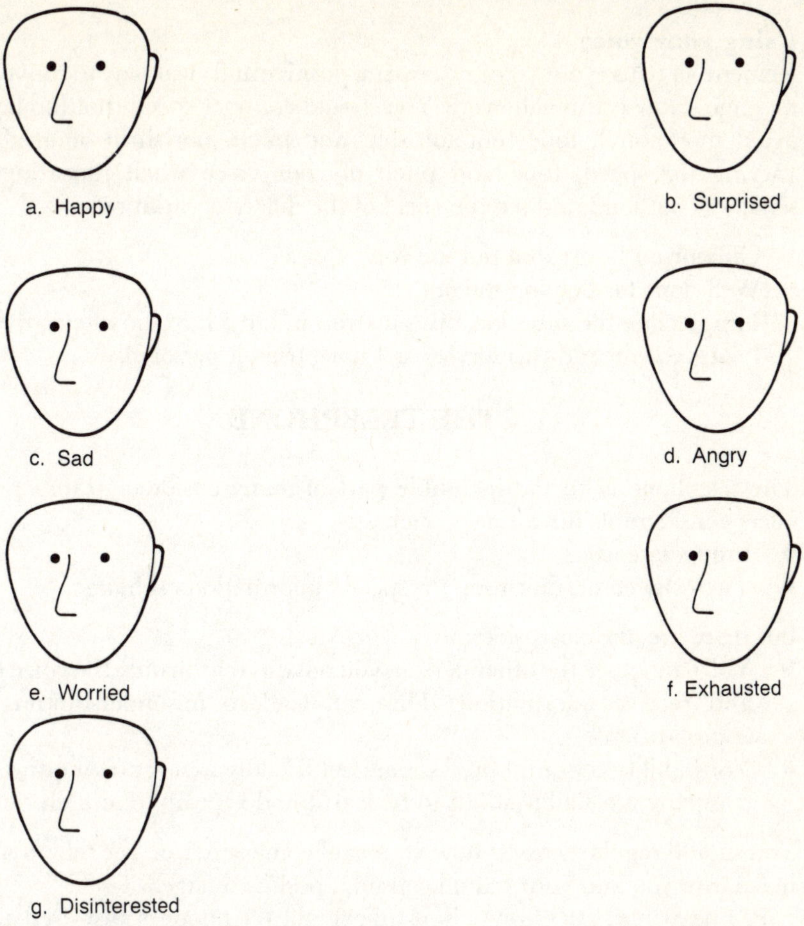

COMMUNICATION AND GETTING THE MESSAGE ACROSS 71

a. Happy

b. Surprised

c. Sad

d. Angry

e. Worried

f. Exhausted

g. Disinterested

Figure 8.3 *Facial expressions to complete*

Friendly

Hostile

Figure 8.4 *Friendly and hostile stances*

Using your voice

Remember to use your voice in a warm, positive and clear way to convey your message. How is this achieved? You should consider speed (not too fast, but avoid monotony), tone (not too soft) and pitch (not shrill or gruff). Try varying the speed, tone and pitch of your voice when repeating these sentences out loud and see the effect of the different variations:

> 'Of course I'll sort that out for you'
> 'Well done for helping me out'
> 'I appreciate the situation this puts you in but I have no alternative'
> 'I can recommend this service as I have tried it personally'

THE TELEPHONE

The telephone is an indispensable part of many customer transactions. It offers considerable advantages, such as:
- Immediate access
- Two-way communication for speedy information exchange.

But there are also downsides:
- You cannot see the other person; you have to rely on only the voice to give and receive information. This can lead to misunderstandings and complications.
- Your ability to sound professional yet friendly as a representative of the company is a skill that has to be learnt and kept up to scratch.

Be alert to the effect on the customer of all forms of communication, whether face to face, on the telephone, through letters and reports, or at meetings.

You should regularly assess how your staff come across on the telephone and make sure you and your team keep up a positive image.

Pay particular attention to how quickly the telephone is answered and the message which is given on answering.

Brief receptionists or people answering the telephone to put customers quickly through to the correct department. Ensure that all members of staff are able to answer the 'phone in a customer-friendly manner and that messages are taken and passed on efficiently.

WRITTEN COMMUNICATION

Written communication by letter, fax, electronic mail or report is valuable as:
- A record, to be referred to later
- A means to study more complex information
- A means of dealing with an issue at the most convenient time.

But because there is no opportunity to check back, it needs care to avoid misunderstanding.

Increasingly the tone and style of written communication with customers is becoming less formal. Language is becoming simpler and more friendly.

Example of customer-friendly letter

Dear Mrs Smith

Thank you for your letter of 20th February.

I am pleased to hear that you wish to extend your product warranty.

I have asked the Customer Service Manager, Tony White, at your local dealer, A J Cox, in Cheltenham to call you. He can arrange to extend the product warranty for you within our special offer period.

I hope you will be happy with the service you receive from A T Cox. Please contact me if you need any further help.

Yours sincerely

John Jones
Customer Contracts Manager

Tips to help you

Here are some tips which should help in writing:
- Marshal your thoughts before you write. What do you want the reader to do as a result of your communication?
- Be brief but friendly.
- Avoid jargon or complicated words.
- Keep sentences short.
- Break up your message into four- or five-sentence paragraphs which are arranged logically. Insert headings and bullet points to make it more readable.
- With longer reports include a summary and action points at the beginning for ease of understanding.

MEETINGS

Clear and effective communication is vital at meetings. Unfortunately most people's experiences at meetings suggest that bad habits can easily creep in. When running a meeting make sure you remember to:
- Be clear what you want to achieve from the meeting and reflect this in the agenda
- Promote the contribution of ideas from everyone

- Encourage plenty of listening; do not allow a meeting to move on if there is a lot of interrupting and squashing of ideas
- Keep the meeting on track
- Have follow-up actions
- Hold regular short meetings rather than infrequent, long meetings.

MAKING PRESENTATIONS

Everyone has to make presentations from time to time. Some people get very nervous about it and do not give of their best. Others become complacent and risk losing the attention of their audience. These reminders will help you to be persuasive and appreciated for your message. Consider them before every presentation.

1. Know your audience. What are they there for? What is their level of knowledge? In presenting to customers, beware of using jargon or talking over their heads, particularly with technical products and services.
2. Define your objective. Is it to inform? to persuade? to gain action?
3. Prepare thoroughly. Usually you should allow seven or eight times as long to prepare as the presentation itself. There is no substitute for a dummy delivery run-through to prepare a presentation, reducing problems on the day and maximising impact.
4. Think about the order of presentation. Ten minutes is about the maximum high attention span, so put your main points early on.
5. Accept that your audience will retain only a small amount of what they are told – repeat key points for emphasis to ensure better retention. Summarise at the end. Keep main points to a maximum of five.
6. To help you deliver confidently but retain audience contact, use summary notes of key headings to act as a reminder.
7. Involve your audience for greater interest and commitment. For example ask, 'How many computers do you maintain?'
8. Some variety of delivery and media helps. For example, during a presentation you might use a flip chart/white board and overhead projector.
9. When using overhead projector slides do not cram too much on one slide – six points maximum, three or four words for each point. A picture speaks a thousand words. You will have more impact with graphical presentation, particularly of figures.
10. Open with something interesting and attention grabbing, close on a high note. People particularly remember the first and last things you say.

When you are delivering your presentation:

Do
- speak slowly and clearly
- pause and look at the audience regularly
- come across with energy and enthusiasm

Don't
- read notes word for word and hide behind them, never looking up
- use distracting mannerisms – hands in pockets, clicking pens etc
- stand in front of an overhead projector
- ramble.

Study also the Checkpoints in Table 8.2.

Table 8.2 *Checkpoints in making a presentation*

Beginning	Middle	End
Open with interesting bait	Make into easily discernible segments	Summarise
Define objectives, structure	Summarise regularly	Positive conclusions
Give background	Involve audience	Point the way to action
	Use clear, uncluttered visual aids	

KEEPING CUSTOMER AND INTERNAL COMMUNICATION LINKS STRONG

Part of the process of communicating with customers is finding appropriate methods for ensuring two-way communication.

As the number of people you deal with gets larger, you need to be more formal and find communication vehicles to gain access to groups readily. This will ensure that you do not lose sight of valuable information and you keep people informed. Below are some suggestions that you may wish to explore to improve communication with your customers, your own team and internal customers in the company.

Communication is two way, so invite feedback from customers, staff and internal customers.

Customers

There are a number of methods you can adopt to gain feedback from customers.

The method which allows the greatest degree of one-to-one feedback is regular visits to customers to see how well you are performing as a company and how you can improve. However, the disadvantage of this form of feedback is the limited number of customers you can visit on a one-to-one basis.

You gain a more representative sample of opinion from customer satisfaction surveys, sent directly to the customer or handed out at point of sale. However, the response levels to such surveys can often be low in comparison with the costs involved. Other methods which can be used to gain feedback from customers include:
- Pre-paid response forms included with the product or information on the services you supply
- In-depth interviews with a sample of typical customers to gain their points of view
- Third-party surveys where independent organisations review the level of service you provide your customers
- Customer focus groups to allow customers to comment on service.

When considering the merits of each method remember to be clear what you are trying to achieve. A combination of different techniques can often be appropriate. For example, customer focus groups will make you more aware of issues of concern to customers which can then be explored with a wider sample of your customers using customer satisfaction questionnaires.

Your own team
Here is a large selection of ideas for improving communication amongst your team. Why not pick out the most promising and discuss them further with your team?
- Give publicity to all examples of excellent practice
- Issue regular reminders of the importance of the customer
- Have service poster slogan campaigns
- Set up employee service groups to introduce and publicise service improvements
- Set up a notice board in the department for service progress and achievements
- Introduce a newsletter
- Implement team briefing – regular updates for all staff on a systematic basis in small teams
- Listen to all employees' concerns and suggestions
- Get out of your office regularly and stay in touch with people
- Make an effort to keep informal links
- Set up consultative staff meetings
- Ensure you carry out one-to-one staff performance review meetings.

Your internal customers in the company

Do not forget to develop communication links with those customers to whom you provide a service within your organisation. (See Chapter 13 on the internal customer for a fuller discussion.)

SUMMARY

- Good managers consider *what* they intend to say, *who* will receive the message, *why* they are communicating, *how* to get their point across and *when* they need to do this.
- In this way they are able to choose the correct medium and put their message across in an appropriate way.
- Effective communication involves:
  - Attentive listening
  - Good use of questions – start with open-ended questions (eg who? what? how?), then be more specific
  - Providing clear explanations
  - Awareness of the effect of non-verbal communication such as body language
  - Good use of voice: warm, positive and clear.
- As the number of people you deal with gets larger, you need to work at setting up and maintaining formal communication channels. This is important in monitoring customer opinion and satisfaction, team communication and for your internal customer links.
- Keeping customer and internal communication strong involves a process of active two-way communication.

EXERCISES

1. Consider two recent cases in your own experience of communications which did not turn out as intended. Give thought to what happened:
   - Who was involved?
   - What was the purpose of the message?

   Assess critically your part in the problem. What would you do next time to avoid such a situation arising again?

   Do the same exercise with your team. Discuss the results with them.

2. Reassess the specific means by which you keep in touch with
   - customers
   - your team
   - other parts of the company.

   Keep a note for a week on how often you have communicated with these groups and rate the outcome of these encounters. What can you learn from these? Is there scope to improve? In

what ways? How do you intend to make improvements? Do you need to re-evaluate your channels of communication?
3. Consider some specific skill areas.

Questioning
Do I ask enough open questions? (Who? What? Why? How?)
Do customers readily grasp the meaning of my questions?
Do I pick up and respond to what people are saying?
Do I put my questions in a courteous and friendly manner?

Listening
Do I take enough time to listen to my customers and colleagues?
Do I successfully identify themes?
Do I pick out what is not said?

Clear explanations
Do I answer customers' queries to their satisfaction?
Am I clear when I give explanations or information to customers and staff members?

Body language
Do I match what I say with how I say it?
Am I aware of other people's non-verbal reactions to what I am saying?

4. Brush up your presentation skills by seeking some feedback from your audience, perhaps by asking someone specifically to do this.
5. Review how you and your team handle customers both on the telephone and in writing. How can these two methods of communication be improved?

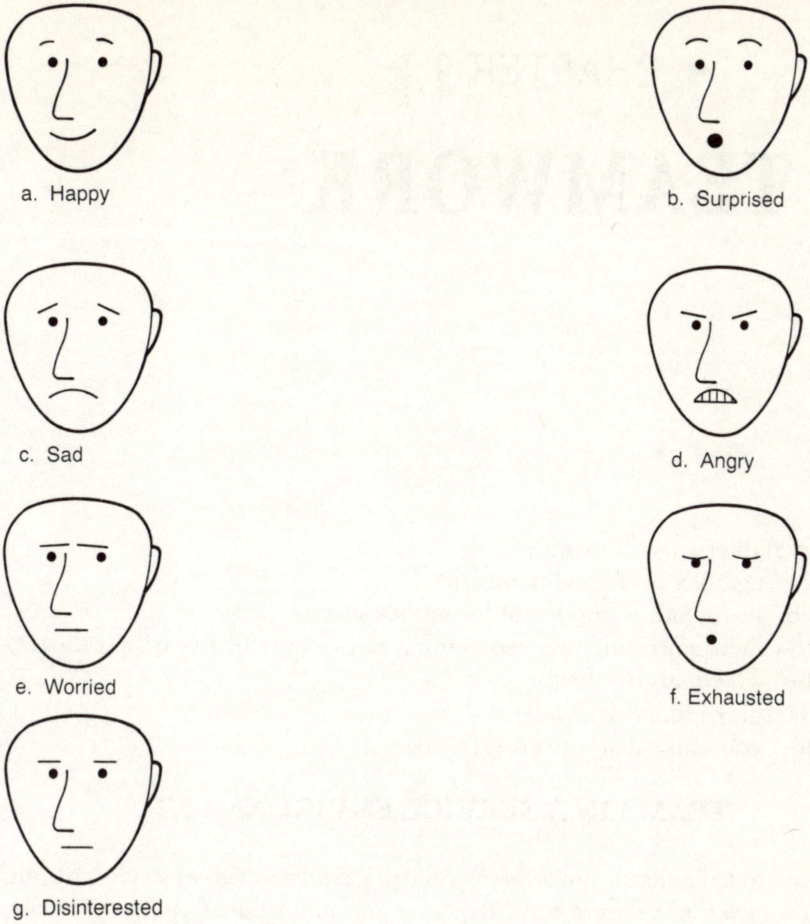

COMMUNICATION AND GETTING THE MESSAGE ACROSS 79

a. Happy

b. Surprised

c. Sad

d. Angry

e. Worried

f. Exhausted

g. Disinterested

Figure 8.5 *Suggestions for completing the expressions in Figure 8.3 (page 71)*

◀ CHAPTER 9 ▶

TEAMWORK

In this chapter we will explore:
- The ingredients of good teamwork
- Why teamwork is important for service success
- How each contributor adds something extra to an effective team – the two plus two equals five factor
- The role of the team leader
- How you make team meetings work well.

TEAMS IN A SERVICE ENVIRONMENT

Good teamwork is immediately apparent to the customer.

Working together as a team is an essential prerequisite of good service. Strong teams, for example, ensure consistency of communication with the customer, deadlines are more likely to be met, and everyone takes responsibility for their actions with no 'finger pointing'.

In the customer's eyes, a weak team shows itself through poor customer service such as the left hand not knowing what the right hand is doing, dates constantly being missed or revised, and a lack of responsibility for action.

Being part of a team does not necessarily mean you have to have the same boss or share the same place of work, though this is common. When you work together as a group of people who share a common objective and recognise that you need the contributions of each member of the group to achieve your objective, this means you are part of an effective team.

In a customer service environment, a team's common objective is often to work together to meet and exceed customers' expectations and to provide a good-quality service through all their efforts coming together to achieve excellence.

THE BENEFITS OF TEAMWORKING

Real teamwork needs careful management and application to develop and maintain the group pride and strength. But once you have got it, it will give you a distinctive edge. It is very noticeable to the customer, in the following ways:
- The workplace is a lively place to be – morale and energy are obviously high
- New ideas are readily coming forward
- There is a friendly atmosphere and people are open with each other
- Information is freely shared and available
- Everyone knows what they have to do and they have the confidence that comes from knowing how they are performing
- The group is supportive and cohesive on the inside which provides a seamless service on the outside; everyone helps each other willingly.

Take a few moments to think about the most effective team you have ever worked in. How many of these characteristics can you identify? Are there others you would pick out to add to this list of the ingredients of good teamwork? Now do the same for the worst team you have worked in. What characteristics have you picked out? Compare your list with the one below.

LACK OF TEAMWORK

The opposite of good teamwork – everyone working as disparate individuals – is usually very apparent to the customer, in the following ways:
- There is a stale atmosphere, with visible muttering, moaning and complaining
- No-one seems to know what is going on outside their own immediate responsibilities – the 'I don't know it's not my job' phenomenon
- There is indifference or animosity when things go wrong
- The organisation is hard to do business with; responsibility always seems to lie with someone else
- The whole operation does not seem to work too well: procedures get out of date, rules are set by people who are out of touch.

HOW DOES YOUR TEAM SHAPE UP?

Try the questions in Table 9.1 among your team members to see how your team shapes up. As a result of analysing the results from Table 9.1, draw up a list of actions you need to initiate to make progress in strengthening your team.

82   LEADING YOUR TEAM RESOURCEFULLY

Table 9.1   *Teamwork questionnaire*

For each pair of statements, score your team 1 or 5 if the statement nearest to the number strongly reflects your view of your team. 2 or 4 are less close but quite strongly reflect your team. 3 is in the middle of the two statements.

We do not really know our customers – who are the key customers, what is their business, who are new customers	1	2	3	4	5	We know our customers well – key customers, new and regular customers
We do not really put ourselves out for the customer	1	2	3	4	5	We will do anything to serve the customer
We are confused about our roles and what is expected	1	2	3	4	5	We know what we have got to do and what is expected of us
We are in the dark about what is going on. We do not know about changes until much too late	1	2	3	4	5	Communication is good – we have regular updates
It is every one for themself round here	1	2	3	4	5	If we need help, people in the team support each other
No one makes suggestions for change; procedures and systems are out of step with reality	1	2	3	4	5	We contribute lots of new ideas on ways to do things
There is a bad atmosphere much of the time	1	2	3	4	5	It is an enjoyable place to work
There is a noticeable lack of some skills in our team	1	2	3	4	5	We have a rounded balance of skills in our team
Some people do not pull their weight	1	2	3	4	5	Everyone makes a full contribution
People are afraid to take responsibility for decisions	1	2	3	4	5	People take full responsibility for decisions
We suppress differences of view and conflict – they sometimes simmer below the surface	1	2	3	4	5	We deal openly with conflict and differences

Scoring

If everything in your team is working well you would score between 40 and 55, 25 or over and you are on the right track, less than 25 and you have plenty of improvement to make.

BALANCE IN A TEAM

There is a lot of truth in the saying, variety is the spice of life, when it comes to the composition of a team. The most effective teams are unlikely to be made up of clones. But some team variations work and other teams do not. Research into effective teams suggests that it is getting the right balance which makes the difference.

What do we mean by balance? We are thinking here not of the specialist functional roles, but the roles people fulfil when working together to achieve the task. Meredith Belbin suggests teams need to get a balance between:

- Leaders who take charge
- Ideas people who come up with bright suggestions
- Implementers good at the practicalities
- Team-orientated people who pay particular attention to other people in the team
- Coordinators who bring it all together
- Analysts who scrutinise the facts
- Finishers who dot the 'i's and cross the 't's
- Outgoing contacts people who 'know a person who can' and soon get help or information when needed.

Teams need the right balance of different contributors to function well.

If you get team role gaps or there are too many preferring a particular role the team is unlikely to function well. This is true even if team members are bright and able as individual contributors.

Belbin believes that each team role has something positive to contribute to making a team effective. Unfortunately each role has a negative side too which needs to be kept in check if the team is to succeed. The ideal team allows the best part of each person's team role to flourish.

Leaders, or shapers as Belbin calls them, do not necessarily have the title, manager or team leader. They want to get things moving, confront and change, sometimes with impatience which rankles with others.

Ideas people, or plants in Belbin's terminology, are unorthodox people who make imaginative suggestions but can put their heads in the clouds and disregard practical detail and protocol.

Outgoing contacts people, or resource investigators in Belbin's terms, always seem to be on the 'phone or talking to someone. Their curiosity and enthusiastic extroversion is very useful for exploring anything new, although they can quickly lose interest and want to move on to explore fresh pastures.

Implementers are dutiful, practical people with plenty of common-sense and who get things done, but they are inclined to be inflexible and cautious of change.

Analysts, or the Belbin term, monitor evaluators, exercise a hard-headed unemotional filter on inconsistent or impractical team actions, although in excess they may be a 'wet blanket' and inclined to pessimism.

Finishers, Belbin's completers/finishers, have a good capacity to follow things through and tie up loose ends, though they need to be watchful that their orderly conscientiousness does not give way to nit-picking and worrying.

Team-orientated people, Belbin's teamworkers, promote team spirit and are sensitive to the people in the team, though they can be indecisive at times of crisis.

Coordinators have a strong sense of the common goal and welcome all contributions on merit without prejudice. They do not shine in intellect or creativity above the others.

A good coordinator harnesses the strength of all team members to ensure that there is balance in the team and that everyone's contribution is valued.

Example
The help-desk in a large company reported to the systems manager. This manager was a contacts person – hands off, no attention to detail, not very interested in routine matters. His profile was not ideal for managing a help-desk although in all other matters relating to his work he was very good.

The help-desk personnel took 'phone calls and dealt with them themselves or passed them on to the relevant programmer or analyst to resolve. They were understaffed and the team leader worked as one of the help-desk staff as well as being the manager of the group. She had been appointed because of her technical expertise and because management recognised her conscientiousness and thorough behaviour – characteristics universally held to be good though not, in this case, at all appropriate in the highly flexible environment and with a boss who was always out and about.

Her team profile was implementer. This meant she was anxious, highly detail conscious, a perfectionist, conservative, cautious and very structured.

The end result was that she could not handle the pressure and get herself organised to her satisfaction. She worried and worried without being able to get on top of anything. She lacked the ability to share her worries with her boss; she saw her boss as not interested in her problems.

Here were two very capable individuals but their team roles were at odds with each other. The end result was poor performance. They had been appointed for their individual strengths with no thought to their team strengths and complementary roles. What was missing in this team was a teamworker or coordinator who would bring balance to the team.

Auditing your team
How does your team look if you assign team roles to each member? Read through the team role descriptions again and tentatively put the names in

your team against the roles. It is likely each will be able to exercise a secondary or back-up role, particularly useful if there are gaps in the team. When you have carried out your analysis ask yourself the questions below and then get your team together to review and discuss how your team functions.

1. Reflect on recent team decisions. Have you found any of the following which might suggest the need to re-examine the roles within your team?
   - A shortage of ideas
   - An inability to build on suggestions
   - Avoidance of making decisions
   - Non-existent or incomplete follow-up for implementing decisions
   - Poor quality decisions.
2. Are there role imbalances? If so, which roles are absent or weak? Which roles are over-represented?
3. What effect is any imbalance causing?
4. What strengthening actions do you need to take within the current team?
5. What roles do you need to add through recruitment when the opportunity arises?

THE ROLE OF THE TEAM LEADER

As the leader of a team, you have a special part to play. Your role is to:
- Provide a framework for achieving the task as a team
- Facilitate the team coming together
- Make sure there is a good flow of information between team members
- Foster a sense of energy, enthusiasm and purpose
- Build a sense of team identity and belonging.

Motivating your team

An important skill of the team leader is knowing what motivates your team. This means recognising how to get the best from your team and how to make certain that everyone feels they have an important contribution to make in serving the customer. There are no magic rules to creating a motivating environment but these tips can help you build the right level of motivation. Use them as a regular checklist.

As a leader you must motivate your team and make sure everyone feels their contribution is important.

- Set clear objectives
- Recognise the positives
- Celebrate success
- Provide feedback on performance – both good and bad
- Seek to constantly improve your own and your team's performance
- Show your appreciation
- Encourage participation and involvement
- Ask your team what motivates them to give that 101 per cent! Take heed of the answers.

When the sparks fly

Naturally in every team there are disagreements and conflicts which arise from working closely together. We are all different in personalities, values and priorities. The more we depend on others, the more likely that it is that differences will occur. Conflict is also an inevitable and likely part of the development of a team. It is said that before a team performs at its best, it needs to have gone through three stages first. The first is getting to know each other, forming. Then comes storming, working out who does what and how. Finally there is the stage of norming, agreeing a code of conduct. This applies to new teams but may also reoccur when large numbers of newcomers join an established team or important changes take place.

Conflict within the team is both inevitable and necessary to work productively for the customer.

Through challenge and conflict, a team can learn and explore together. Your role as a team leader is to manage conflict purposely. Do not be afraid of conflict within the group; recognise this as a positive and healthy sign. It is unresolved conflict which drags a team down. You should:

- Encourage everyone to say what they think and feel and talk out differences. Be an example for the rest of the team.
- Develop the skills of feedback in your team. It is often not just what you say, but how you say it which can conversely cause offence or promote beneficial changes.
- When you spot differences which are not being resolved, act as a go-between to iron out problems. This means allowing both parties to let off steam, making certain that both are listening to the points made, then you can usefully summarise where you are and press for conclusions and actions.

SUGGESTIONS FOR IMPROVING A SERVICE TEAM

All teams benefit from constantly reviewing their performance. In serving the customer, teams must learn better ways and sharpen their skills if they are not to be overtaken by smarter competitors who practise continuous improvement. Here are some ideas to help this process.

- Make sure everyone knows their customers and their needs. Perhaps arrange visits or introductions when customers visit you. This keeps a single common focus, the customer.
- Keep people informed through regular communications meetings. Keep these short but tailored to what your team is interested in and what it needs to know.
- Give regular feedback on how each person is performing. Examples might be the results of customer surveys, letters received from customers on the quality of service, costs for the month, output from the department. Many companies find a service noticeboard useful, placed in a visible place with regular performance and information updates.
- Set clear service standards and objectives and monitor and jointly review individual and group performance against them. Involve staff in setting these.
- Encourage suggestions and ideas for improvements. Often the people who know are those who

operate the procedures day by day. Every few months hold a review meeting to take a wider look at how things are going. Use it to boost spirits as well as inform.
- In recruiting new staff be sensitive to how that person will fit into the team as well as the individual contribution they will make.
- Deal with conflict openly and fairly. Encourage a cooperative, supportive approach to each other. It is easy to find fault, not so easy to listen to other people and to find positive things to say.
- Encourage knowledge and understanding of each other's jobs to give the team flexibility. This also builds cooperation and breaks down selfishness. Some job rotation can help here. Also consider asking individuals to share particular expertise with others.
- Set up small task groups on particular problems. This will have the spin-off of building team spirit.
- Occasionally organise out-of-work events to cement team spirit.
- Keep a close watch on team morale, which is prone to dip in pressured service environments. If it does, remind people of the things that are going right too, and help resolve outstanding issues.
- Take particular care to introduce new team members by setting clear standards, offering appropriate training and encouraging a welcoming atmosphere. Consider asking an experienced team member to become a mentor, giving the newcomer the benefit of their advice and coaching them.

MEETINGS

Informal and formal meetings are a key means of promoting teamwork. They need good chairing and willing and effective participation from everyone. Reread the section on meetings in Chapter 8 to remind yourself of tips which will help to get a meeting to work for you and your team.

SUMMARY

- Working in teams is an effective and proven means of providing consistently excellent customer service – see Figure 9.1.
- A good team has a balance of roles, communicates openly and freely and is a supportive and cohesive group.
- The role of the team leader is to provide a framework for the team, organise its efforts, ensure good communication, motivate the team, and resolve problems and conflict.
- Effective teams constantly review and improve their performance.
- Short well-run meetings promote teamwork and should be held on a regular basis.

88 LEADING YOUR TEAM RESOURCEFULLY

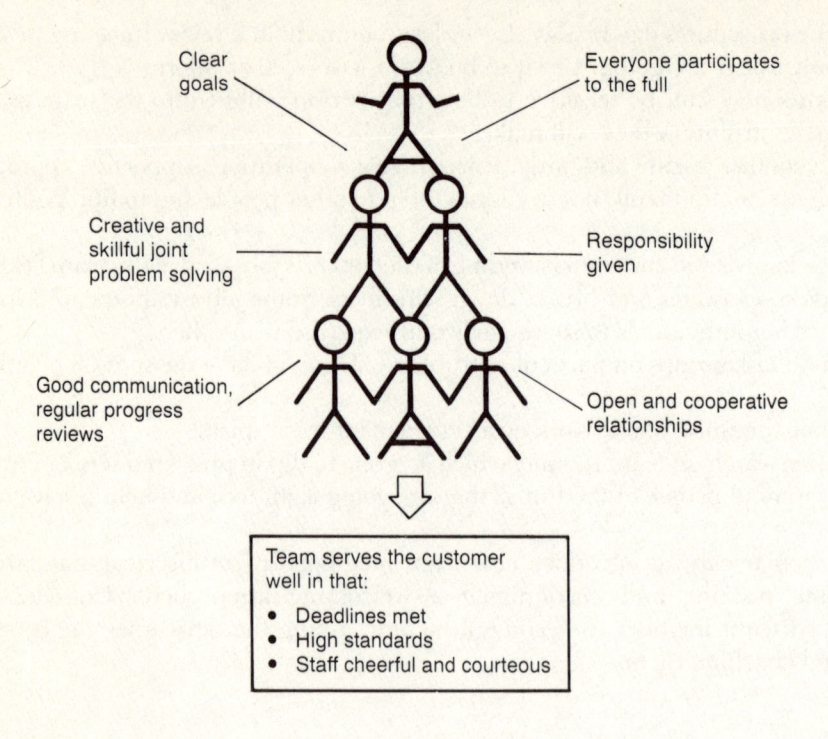

Figure 9.1 *How teamwork serves the customer*

Labels around figure:
- Clear goals
- Everyone participates to the full
- Creative and skillful joint problem solving
- Responsibility given
- Good communication, regular progress reviews
- Open and cooperative relationships

Team serves the customer well in that:
- Deadlines met
- High standards
- Staff cheerful and courteous

HOW TO GET BETTER AT TEAMWORK

1. Start by conducting a review of how well your team works. Test the temperature by asking:
   - Is everyone participating?
   - Do all team members turn up for meetings?
   - Is everyone clear about goals?
   - How up to date are people on what is going on?
   - How happy and energetic is the climate?
2. Assess critically your last two team meetings. Rate honestly the strengths and weaknesses of that meeting. What were the causes of each? What could be done to improve meetings in future? Target your next meeting to get started in improving matters.
3. Summarise by feeding back to your team:
   - *Three* things you are going to *start* doing
   - *Three* things you are going to *stop* doing
   - *Three* things you intend to *continue* promoting and doing.

   Ask for comments and suggestions. Consider inviting each team member to follow your lead and do the same.

◀ CHAPTER 10 ▶

RECRUITMENT AND SELECTION

This chapter considers:
- What factors influence the effectiveness of a recruitment and selection procedure
- What preparations you need to make before recruiting
- What makes a good interview
- What role you play in ensuring you choose the right candidate.

To choose a high-quality candidate for their team, a manager must make an effort to be thorough in the whole recruitment and selection process. It will add value because a good contributor is likely to fit in well with the team, put something into it and make a positive contribution towards the customer. A poor one may disrupt the group, sap morale or make extra work for the manager or other people and provide poor service to the customer.

HOW DO YOU RECRUIT AND SELECT A CANDIDATE?

It is important that your recruitment and selection is soundly based. If you were interviewing for the position of receptionist within your own company and had shortlisted three candidates, which one of those in Table 10.1 would you select? Write down all the steps which led to your decision and the relative importance of each. Ask a colleague to do the same and compare your answers.

90 LEADING YOUR TEAM RESOURCEFULLY

Table 10.1 *Sample job candidate shortlist*

Candidate one :	21 years old
Previous experience :	Receptionist/telephonist at Global International for three years.
Reason for leaving :	Prefers a smaller company.
General information :	Strong accent but clear diction, friendly, bubbly personality. Average neatness. Explained at interview that she suffers from asthma and wishes to work in a smoke-free environment.
Hobbies :	Dancing, member of Territorial Army.
Candidate two :	27 years old
Previous experience :	Help-desk administrator in customer services department of credit card company for four years. Prior to this receptionist/telephonist for five years with local company.
Reason for leaving :	Redundant
General information :	Appeared good all-rounder. Brightly dressed with a lot of jewellery. Stated at interview that she was looking for a job with career prospects and promotion opportunities.
Hobbies :	Cooking, leader of cub pack, voluntary leader of one-parent family group.
Candidate three :	46 years old
Previous experience :	Currently working within your company as an assistant administrator. Has been with the company for 13 years and has a good knowledge of products. Is known to be a bit of a ringleader within her department.
Reason for leaving :	To be more busy. General information : Quietly spoken, appears very conscientious, likes paperwork and administration. Is always smartly dressed.
Hobbies :	Gardening, embroidery, amateur dramatics

You may well have found some discrepancies between what you have decided and the decision of your colleagues. Exploring this further, you may find that the assumptions on which you based your decision were different. To provide a consistent and systematic method, it is important to have a thorough approach. We have set out one below.

THE STAGES IN RECRUITMENT

1. Do you need to fill the job?

Check that you still have a need to fill the job and what that need is. Often your first thought is to take on a person in the same mould as the last. But the environment is changing so fast today. Take a step back first and ask whether you should reorganise, simplify or combine roles and tasks.

2. What is the job?

Analyse the requirements of the job. What are you asking the job holder to do? What measures of performance do you have to indicate success in performing the role? A job description helps you sort out what you are looking for. It should contain:
- job title
- to whom job holder reports
- objectives of the job
- key tasks
- standards
- dimensions of job (people, money, equipment)
- impact of the job on the organisation
- special conditions, constraints
- an organisation chart or family tree.

3. Who is the person you need?

You need critically to assess what are the capability requirements of the job that a person should meet. A useful way to think of this is in terms of knowledge, skill, behaviours and motivation/attitude. These can be assembled into a person specification.

You need to assess these into 'musts' and 'wants': what you must have as a minimum to do the job, what would be desirable. Try and be realistic here – it is tempting to aim too high and put too many 'musts' down.

For all customer contact people you need to pay particular attention to:
- clarity of communication
- ability to work under pressure
- friendly, approachable manner
- good organisation and priority management.

Divide the capability requirements of a job vacancy into 'musts' and 'wants'.

4. How do you attract the right candidates?

You should consider:
1. *Internal candidates.* This is valuable to demonstrate career development in the company.
2. *External advertisement.* Ensure your advertisement has an accurate description of the job and candidate requirements. Decide whether to include a reference to salary. Say something about the company and its location and how candidates should apply to you. Consider where best to place the job advert – specialist journals, local or national newspapers – according to your budget and the need to reach the appropriate candidates. Remember that the advertisement you place creates an impression of the organisation on potential candidates *and* your customers.

3. *Employment agencies.* Working closely with a limited number of agencies is a preferable route as they will get to know the company and its special needs and address your specialist market.
4. *Head hunters or search consultants.* These are used for hard-to-fill vacancies.

5. Pre-selection

It would usually be impractical to interview everyone, so you need to shortlist candidates for interview and further scrutiny. The clearer your job description and person specification, the easier this will be.

When reading CVs and applications, look carefully at job history and continuity of dates. Examine reasons for leaving positions, how long someone stayed in a role and salary progression. Do any patterns emerge? Look also for other relevant factors such as location, special circumstances, health. A well-designed questionnaire or application form can help you to pick out key information.

Sort applicants into three groups – unsuitable, possible, to be invited for interview.

6. The interview

What is the purpose of the interview? Firstly to discover information about a candidate and to allow you to decide who best matches your needs. But also, importantly, to create goodwill for the company by treating all candidates professionally and selling the company to the candidate.

An interview can be used to create goodwill towards your company as well as for finding out about a candidate.

INTERVIEW PITFALLS

Do you recognise any of these common things said by interviewers?

'I can tell good candidates as soon as they walk in the door'
Research shows that interviewers, particularly untrained interviewers, make up their minds about a candidate's suitability only four minutes into the interview. A careful and systematic approach is required to avoid these instant judgements and to remain as objective as possible.

'Interviewers worth their salt can turn a candidate round in 20 minutes or so'
A well-prepared interviewer can usually glean sufficient information in 30–60 minutes; any less and you risk missing information, any more and you risk rambling and not using anyone's time wisely. But obviously there are no hard and fast rules. Communication at interview is not one way. The interview is also an important opportunity for the candidate to assess the company.

'I always see a candidate three or four times'
Seeing a candidate several times can be useful, particularly in different settings or with different

RECRUITMENT AND SELECTION

people. For high risk or senior jobs this is vital. But do not start to turn the candidate off by too many visits. You may be masking your indecision.

'I relax candidates and they spill the beans'
Generally you will get more information in a relaxed, unhurried atmosphere. But no candidate will be completely open. It is not really a casual conversation.

'I put candidates under stress – after all the job is pressured'
Rarely, if ever, is this justified. It does not simulate real job conditions.

'I always "play it by ear". I don't believe in interview planning and structures'
Some structure gives you the means to compare one candidate with another. But you should not be so rigid that you will only ask pre-determined questions in a certain order.

'I interview on the job at my desk – after all that's the area where they'll be working'
Too many distractions or interruptions during the interview will reduce your ability to get sufficient information from the candidate. Of course, it is helpful to let the candidate see the work environment – but after or before the interview.

'I enjoy interviews'
Some interviewers do. In fact they can turn them into purposeless chats. But equally, many find them quite stressful – after all a lot hangs on your ability to ask the right questions.

'I always interview alone'
While one-to-one interviews can build rapport, you may risk missing vital questions or fail to spot important points. It is preferable to ask at least one other person to interview a candidate to get a different perspective.

'I get a gut feeling about candidates. I'm usually right'
Intuition certainly plays a part in selection. It is not entirely a rational explicit process: personal chemistry is important, even if you cannot always place a definite factual reason for your hunch. But you are on firmer ground if you elicit the facts to back up your hunches.

'I like to set up a good guy/bad guy situation – one tough interviewer and a nice friendly person'
This can be confusing for the candidate and give a poor impression of the company, so tread carefully if you intend to adopt this approach.

'I never pry'
Only questions relevant to the job should be asked, but it is important to ask questions to resolve doubts.

'I don't have prejudices which get in the way of recruitment'

We all have prejudices. Be aware of them. Check out with others where you have blind spots so that you can be particularly watchful of the effect of these at interview. Equal opportunities legislation makes it mandatory that you do not single out a particular group or candidate for questioning on issues you do not raise with all applicants. One example would be asking a woman candidate if she intends to start a family, but not a man.

How do you know whether you've found out enough about a candidate?

Interviewing is a skill which requires careful practice.

Interviewing is a skill which requires careful practice. Having identified the qualities you are seeking within the potential job holder, you need to be able to spot these in potential candidates. The art here is to:

- Ask for evidence of specific skill areas
- Use good questions to get good answers.

There are four question types which are suitable in an interview.

1. *Open questions*. These can be used to open up a topic: 'Tell me about . . .', 'What did you do?'
2. *Probing questions*, which can be used to find out more about a particular issue: 'You say you didn't like your last job. Why is that?', 'What happened then?'
3. *Reflective questions*. These reflect back what the speaker has said to obtain further information: 'You seem unhappy about that.', 'So you're saying you prefer face-to-face contact with customers rather than on the 'phone?'
4. *Closed questions*, which require a single answer and can be used to obtain confirmation or agreement: 'Have you brought along your certificate?', 'So you can start in a month's time?'

Avoid the following unproductive questions:

- *Leading questions*, which force candidates into agreeing with you: 'So you like telephone work then, don't you'.
- *Multiple questions*. You will not obtain a full answer to each of the questions you ask if you pose your questions all in one go: 'So how long did you stay in your first job? Were you happy there? Why did you move on?'

Typical errors in interviewing

A poor interview tends to result from the following behaviour:

- Lack of preparation
- Talking too much and not listening to the candidate
- The interviewer giving their own opinions and judgements
- Asking leading or multiple questions
- Asking challenging questions too early in the interview

- Not getting at the facts or the issues
- Not summarising points
- Wasting time with irrelevancies.

Some do's and don'ts

Do
- Know your candidate's name
- Be prepared – highlight areas you wish to explore, eg gaps in dates between jobs
- Listen carefully throughout
- Probe – Why? How?
- Try and keep an open mind
- Record your impressions and important information
- Give sufficient information about the job and company
- Let candidates know when they will hear from you.

Don't
- Keep the candidate waiting
- Exaggerate the attractiveness of the job
- Rely on your memory to recall everything later
- Take a structure to extremes, either going through a point-by-point structure rigidly or wandering aimlessly with no structure at all
- Talk too much, frequently interrupt
- Display inattentiveness, – ie yawning, looking at your watch, looking away or fail to concentrate on the candidate.

Are there better ways to select than an interview?

Alternative selection methods are becoming more common as a supplement to interviews. Psychometric tests are increasingly being used to measure ability and personality. They need professional specialist advice to ensure that they are the appropriate tests for the selection you have in mind and they are interpreted correctly. You can be trained to administer and interpret certain occupational tests. It is preferable to use questionnaires approved by the British Psychological Society as these are capable of achieving what is claimed and are more consistent in use.

Other methods of selection enable you to observe how people perform in relevant aspects of a role. These include simulating aspects of the job such as answering a 'phone call, doing a keyboard test for example. More sophisticated simulation methods take place in assessment centres, which replicate a variety of work situations and need to be carefully set up in the first instance by experts in this field.

7. Completing the recruitment process

Offer an appointment. An offer letter is a legally binding document. To give yourself leeway it is suggested you make the offer subject to satisfactory references and a medical examination.

Keep in touch with successful candidates before they start in order to keep them interested in the company and so that you can answer any queries.

Remember to make sure that the letter you send to unsuccessful candidates still creates a positive image of the organisation. Reread all rejection letters before they are sent to make sure you are not giving personal affront in what you say to unsuccessful candidates at a sensitive time.

Finally, be aware that recruitment and selection procedures must conform with the law, particularly on discrimination. Read up elsewhere on the law as it applies to this area.

Recruitment and selection must conform with the law, particularly as regards discrimination.

SUMMARY

- The effective recruitment and selection of high-quality employees needs to be a thorough and well thought-out process. This is particularly so where staff are visible to customers.
- See the recruitment process as an opportunity to present your company in the best light.
- Think through what the job entails, who is needed and how you will attract the right candidate. Put this on paper as a person specification and job description.
- Prepare for the interview well and know what you wish to explore. Prepare opening comments and possible questions beforehand.
- Use good questioning in interview situations to ensure full answers which tell you what you need to know. Listen carefully to what you hear. Take note of key points.
- Remember that the process does not finish once a candidate has been selected. Ensure that your follow-up communication creates a positive image of the organisation to both successful and unsuccessful candidates.

EXERCISES

1. Prepare a list of questions for your next interview which will ensure you establish as much as possible about the candidate's career to date, their current job, why they are applying for that job, their interests, personal characteristics and qualities and career aspirations.
2. Hire a camcorder and work with a couple of colleagues to each carry out a practice interview. Review your performance on the video. Quiz your colleagues about ways you can improve. Consider such issues as:
   - adequate coverage

- amount of listening
- questioning technique.

Notice how it felt to be a candidate. It is a worthwhile experience to put yourself in the interviewee's shoes.

3. Review your recruitment and selection track record over the last year (or other shorter period). How are the new staff performing now? How many have left? Check back over your interview notes. What can you learn from these? Talk to each person you selected and ask them what they remember about the interview process, good points and bad.

◀ CHAPTER 11 ▶

PERFORMANCE MANAGEMENT

This chapter addresses some important questions which you as a manager must ask to ensure that you harness the power of your team and deliver superior customer service. These questions are:
- How do you encourage excellence without peering over people's shoulders?
- How do you ensure motivation and commitment?
- How should you conduct performance reviews and appraisals?
- How do you measure performance? How do you reward it?
- What strategies should you adopt to manage differences in individual performance?

We will deal with these questions through exploring the concept of performance management.

WHAT IS PERFORMANCE MANAGEMENT?

It is an approach to management which seeks to harness and focus employee performance on the customer. The visible sign of performance management is that each member of a team is able to answer these questions:
- What is expected of me?
- How am I doing?
- What shall I do next?
- What help do I need to do better?

Performance management gives you, as a manager, the means to implement your responsibilities and goals in serving the customer. It ensures that the components of your team's performance interlock to get the best for the customer. As shown in Figure 11.1, performance management involves a cycle of clarifying business goals and then agreeing individual objectives and standards of performance. With coaching and development, good performance is possible. This will contribute to customer service success, which triggers the cycle of setting further goals and objectives.

HOW DOES GOOD PERFORMANCE MANAGEMENT BENEFIT CUSTOMER SERVICE?

It provides a basis on which to manage staff effectively and to deliver quality service to the customer, because everyone is working to their full capacity and pulling in the same direction. In particular, managing the performance of your team effectively will bear fruit through:

- *Accountability* – everyone knows who does what
- *Quality improvements* – performance targets are well defined and capable of measurable improvement
- *Good communication* – there is a clearly identifiable means of discussing performance
- *Achievement* can be readily recognised and rewarded.

For a team to perform well, everyone in it should be working to their full capacity and pulling in the same direction.

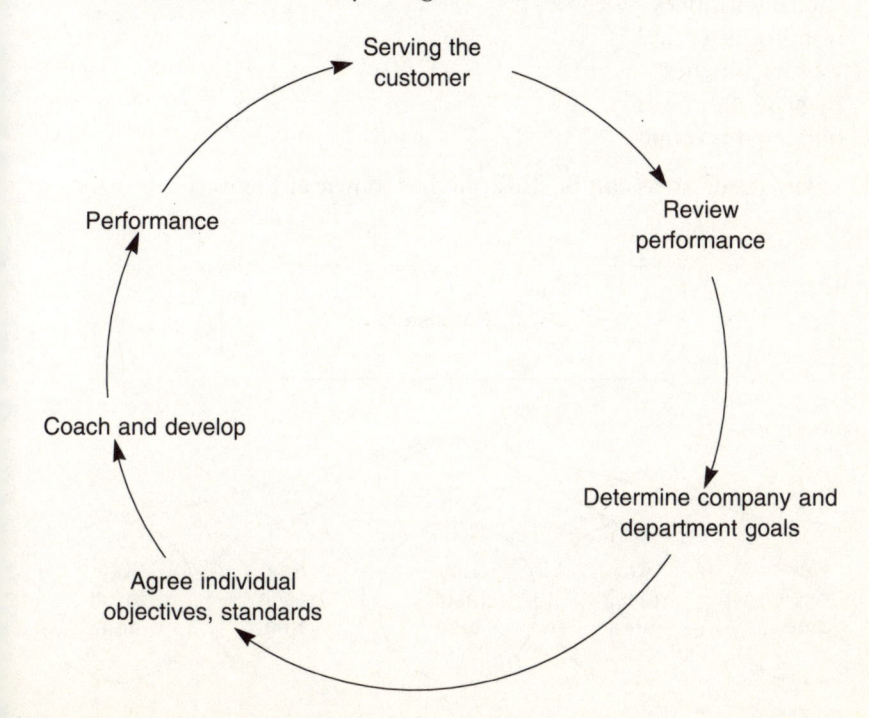

Figure 11.1 *The performance management cycle*

KEY RESULT AREAS

Define the 'key result areas' of each job – the four to eight major things it delivers.

Conditions for success in performance management are:
- An atmosphere of respect and support, so that communication is open and feedback is regularly given
- A definite link between performance and reward
- Both the manager and his or her staff are committed to identified goals.

Performance management enables everyone to know what they are doing and how they are doing against defined yardsticks. It provides clarity between a manager and his or her staff. This clarity starts by getting down to fundamentals. For each job you should ask: why does this job exist? what is its primary purpose? what are the key services I am providing to others? The answers to these questions allow you to define key result areas – what uniquely the job holder is responsible for. For most jobs you can group all the activities someone performs under a few major headings. There are usually about four to eight key outputs or major things you deliver to others. Typical key result areas for a restaurant manager might be the provision of:
- catering supplies
- restaurant services
- visitors' lunches
- hygiene standards
- budgeted revenue.

These key result areas can be illustrated as shown in Figure 11.2.

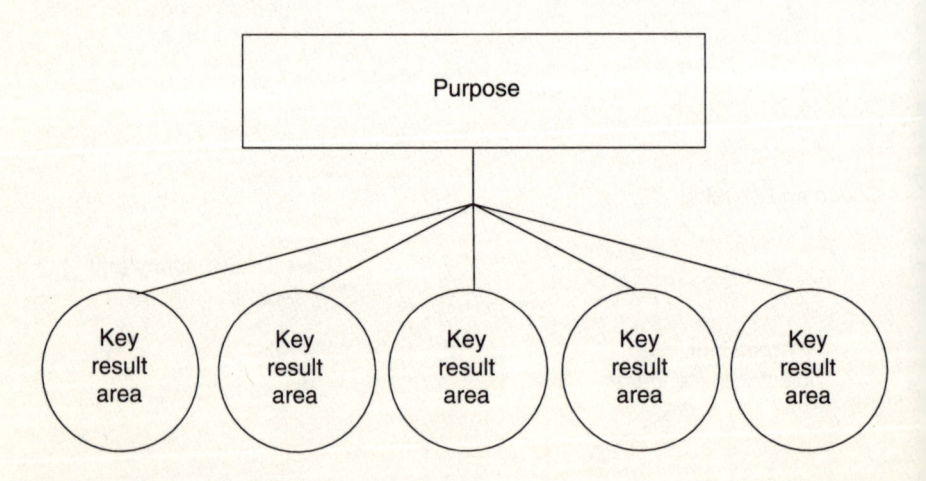

Figure 11.2 *Key result areas*

Key result areas are made clearer by defining standards or measures which provide indicators of success. Indicators to measure key result areas include levels of customer complaints, backlog of work, response times, value of service contracts, unit cost per employee. A manager would normally start with an analysis of their own job to set an overall picture and then work on each role within the team.

SETTING OBJECTIVES

To achieve results against these key result areas, objectives should be set which address the priorities of the moment. Typically such objectives cover three- to twelve-month timeframes. To be effective, objectives need to be *smart*, that is:

- **S**pecific
- **M**easurable
- **A**chievable
- **R**elevant
- **T**ime-bound.

Work out specific objectives for the next three to twelve months.

Table 11.1 is an example of an ill-defined objective, compared with a more explicit and useful objective.

Table 11.1 *Sample 'smart' objective compared to a 'woolly' one*

Smart objective	Woolly objective
By next April, reduce complaints by 15% from level at 15 November, measured by quarterly customer survey and letters received	Reduce customer complaints

The number of objectives set will vary from job to job. Six is about the maximum in any job. It is better not to set too many objectives otherwise you will lose their main benefit which is to pinpoint the most important priorities.

HOW DO YOU MAKE PERFORMANCE MANAGEMENT WORK IN PRACTICE?

Commitment is the key here. Make sure you are prepared to follow a performance management system through and involve your staff all along the line. If you are prepared to waive the objectives aside at the first sign of a crisis, you will fail to make them 'stick' – a common problem with implementing objective setting as a management tool. But this does not mean pressing on with out-of-date objectives regardless. In these times of change be sensitive to the need to review and modify objectives in line with new business requirements and to set new priorities.

MOTIVATION AND PERFORMANCE

Imagine you face the motivational challenge of a manager of a busy customer service department. How do you ensure that customers receive a consistently high standard of service?

Good performance will only come from well-motivated staff. As a manager this means having a good understanding of people's needs and the part work provides in meeting those needs. It means creating an environment where team members can turn to you and each other for encouragement and support.

Everyone has needs to satisfy and some important ones relate to work. Your job as a manager is to help engender the right climate to satisfy these so that your team makes that extra effort to lift and sustain good performance. This will translate itself into customer satisfaction.

If you fail to do this then performance will suffer. Signs of lack of motivation in a team include apathy and indifference, poor performance and poor timekeeping, uncooperative attitudes and unwillingness to change. Each of these have profound implications for serving the customer; the bored look, the slow pace, the indifferent shrug are signs of a death watch beetle gnawing away at the fabric of an organisation.

Figure 11.3 is a simplified diagram of motivation and performance.

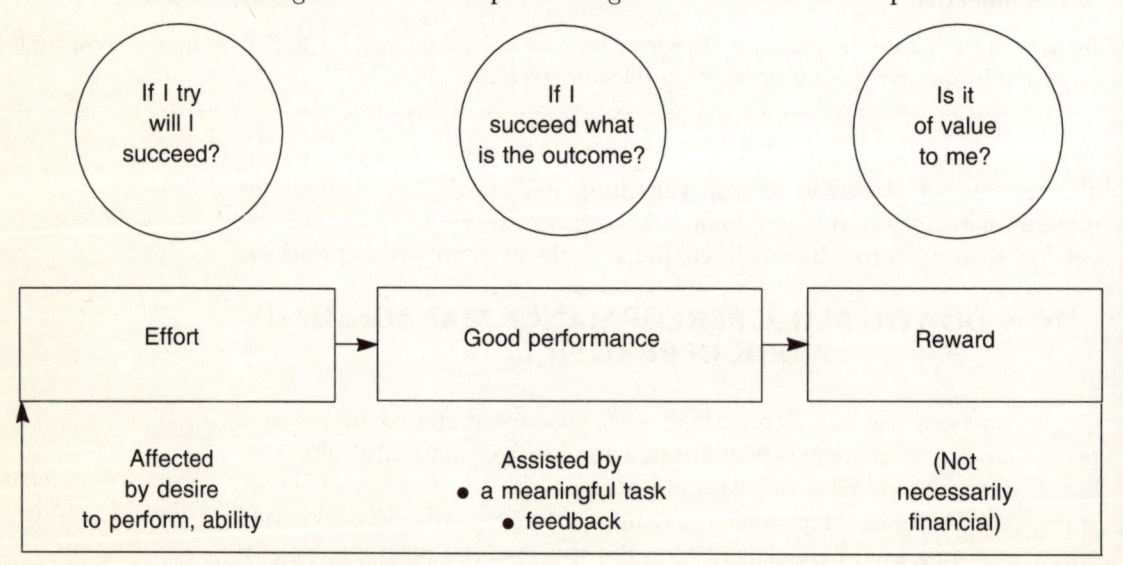

```
   If I try              If I               Is it
   will I             succeed what         of value
   succeed?          is the outcome?        to me?


┌──────────────┐    ┌──────────────────┐    ┌──────────────┐
│    Effort    │───▶│ Good performance │───▶│   Reward     │
└──────────────┘    └──────────────────┘    └──────────────┘

    Affected            Assisted by              (Not
    by desire        • a meaningful task      necessarily
 to perform, ability     • feedback            financial)
```

Figure 11.3 *Motivation and performance*

Maslow's theory of motivation

There is a wide range of theories on what motivates people. One that has proved useful to many managers was put forward by the behavioural scientist, Abraham Maslow. He said that we all have needs to satisfy, but what is uppermost will depend on where we are in a ladder or hierarchy of needs with basic needs of food and shelter near the base and self-respect and self-fulfilment at the top, as shown in Figure 11.4. He argued that when the basic needs of food, shelter and so on had been fulfilled people naturally progress to higher order needs. When any of the basic needs are threatened, people may turn to these again as a primary motivator. You will be less worried about how fulfilling your job is if its very existence is threatened and hence your means to live.

Good performance will only come from well-motivated staff, but different people are motivated by different things.

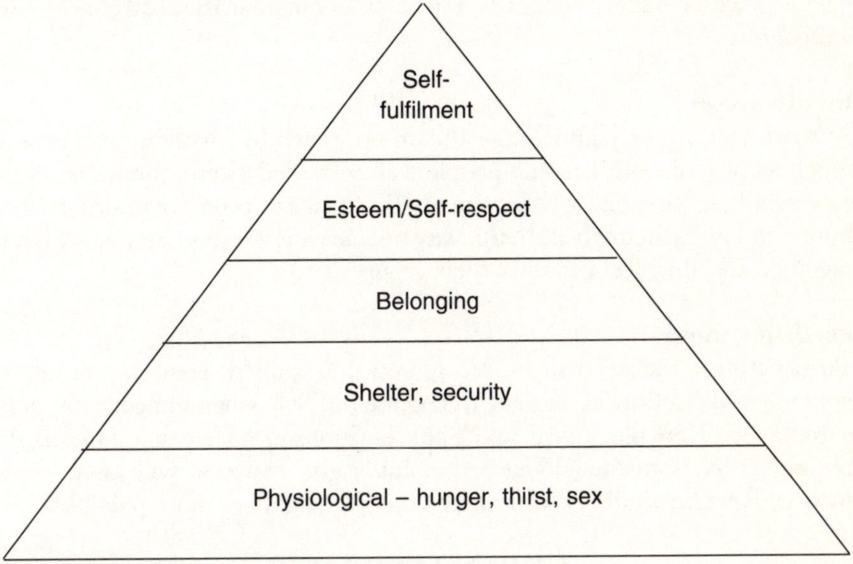
Self-
fulfilment
Esteem/Self-respect
Belonging
Shelter, security
Physiological – hunger, thirst, sex

Figure 11.4 *The hierarchy of needs*

WHAT DOES THIS MEAN TO THE MANAGER?

Pay

At a basic level you need to provide a fair day's work for a decent reward. If you are paying below the market rate it will probably be harder to achieve extra effort, unless there are other strong compensatory factors. The question of pay and its effect on performance will be discussed in more detail later in the chapter, but money is a very tangible and important motivator to satisfy the needs that Maslow talks about.

Security

This is another basic requirement. It means that the more insecure people feel beyond a certain point, the less willing they are to change or to be very productive. Whilst no one can give predictions with certainty in an uncertain world, the least you should aim for is to keep people well informed of the business situation and to avoid nasty surprises. Spell out clear objectives and remove excessive ambiguity or overlap in roles so as to give a greater sense of security.

Belonging

This is one strong motivational need that you can address by encouraging your group to feel a sense of identity and belonging. You should do everything you can to help promote this through birthday celebrations, business review meetings with a buffet afterwards, a department team in the local charity run, a meal out.

Involvement

At work you can help encourage a team approach by involving everyone as much as possible and keeping people well informed. Some companies have successfully set up employee service quality teams to promote improvements from employees themselves. In this way people work because they enjoy being together and they feel proud of their group.

Feeling valued

To help meet the need to be recognised and valued, create a climate of noticing and celebrating success. Recognise publicly when someone has done a good job. Ken Blanchard and Spencer Johnson have made famous the phrase 'catch someone doing something right'. Success will often breed success. Regular feedback will make even the negatives more palatable.

GIVING FEEDBACK

Giving feedback is part and parcel of performance management. It can be an important motivator; it is the means to set standards and correct or encourage performance. Consider the following situation.

One of your team has failed to show up at your task force meetings, despite reminders. On each occasion he has been late back from lunch. You feel annoyed about this as his contribution on his specialist area was missed. What do you say?

1. 'Why didn't you turn up to our meeting. You made me a laughing stock!'
2. Nothing, but glower at him instead.
3. Make sarcastic comments – 'Enjoyable lunch was it?'

4. 'I really appreciate your contributions to the meeting. I felt very let down when you didn't turn up. What was the problem?'

Each of these may have consequences on future performance, as follows.
1. The person may feel accused, put on the spot and blamed without being given a proper chance to defend himself.
2. The message may be misinterpreted or ignored. Certainly the employee will not know what he needs to do in the future and why.
3. This may make the manager feel good, but such indirect comments are vague and belittling to the receiver.
4. This approach stands the best chance of success. It describes how you feel about the person's behaviour and looks to putting things right.

Giving feedback is a constructive way of helping to encourage or change behaviour by letting people know where they stand in a positive, specific and open way.

People need feedback and if you say it correctly you can tell them what they do wrong as well as what they do right.

Giving negative feedback and praising

Managers often find it difficult to give negative feedback on substandard performance. Here are some useful guidelines.
1. Start with the positive. It is helpful for someone to be reminded that you notice and value their strengths.
2. Be specific. For example, not 'your presentation was poor', but 'your presentation lasted half an hour and the audience lost interest and didn't ask any questions'.
3. Comment on what the person can change. It is no use asking someone to correct a stammer for example.
4. Focus on performance not the person. For example instead of 'you're abrupt with customers' try 'customers often find you don't give them enough time to explain their problem'.
5. Be factual; do not jump in with a judgement straight away. For example, rather than 'you were wrong to put the complaint on hold', try 'when you put the complaint on hold, the customer didn't know what was happening'.
6. Look for ways forward and how to correct the problem in the future.
7. Give feedback soon after the event while memories are fresh.

In praising, a similar process is useful.
1. Be specific and relate it to the performance not the person.
2. State the positive consequences of doing the job well.
3. Give praise quickly after the positive performance to reinforce the behaviour.

CONDUCTING PERFORMANCE REVIEW MEETINGS

Regular performance reviews provide an opportunity for managers and the people who work for them to have an open and honest discussion on their performance at work. Performance reviews are based on the philosophy that people cannot learn and develop unless they receive feedback on how they are performing. Feedback should be regular and timed near to the event. But there is still room to take stock more fully at an appraisal or performance review.

When performance reviews are conducted well they are constructive and motivating. They should not, however, be a substitute for daily contact by the manager nor for regular feedback on performance.

Common pitfalls in conducting performance reviews

There are a number of typical errors which managers often make when conducting a performance review:
- Poor preparation
- Inadequate briefing of employees
- Assessment of personality, not behaviour
- Talking too much
- Failing to probe and sift out what is fact and what is opinion
- Avoiding issues
- Failing to support what is said with examples
- Not enough time for the discussion
- Poor venue
- Interruptions
- Carrying out a performance review at the same time as a salary review, so that how much someone is paid dominates the discussion.

How to conduct a successful performance review

1. Prepare beforehand. Select examples of different kinds of performance, of good, poor and average. Think about the most appropriate style for the discussion – telling, joint approach, consultative, largely self appraisal.
2. For major reviews, give plenty of notice – at least a week – to allow the employee time to prepare.
3. Confirm understanding of the purpose of the review, which is improvement not blame.
4. Ensure a quiet, uninterrupted setting.
5. At the review start in a positive, receptive manner. Agree the agenda.
6. Listen carefully and summarise regularly, checking joint understanding.
7. Do not hold a defensive post-mortem; look forward to what you can do to make things better in the future. Cover all aspects of performance –

good, bad and average and certainly do not just dwell on problems.
8. At the end, summarise each key point. Check understanding and commitment. End on a positive note.
9. Do what you have agreed to do by way of follow-up action.

STRATEGIES FOR DEALING WITH INDIVIDUAL PERFORMANCE

Every employee and every situation needs to be treated individually. However, in dealing with certain types of behaviour, you may find the following strategies a useful starting point.

The poor performer
One of your team when under pressure is aggressive on the 'phone to customers. You have received two complaints. Each requires you to speak to the individual and give feedback. You need to approach the situation carefully, but you need him to change his behaviour. What do you do?
- Say 'What's up with you? I keep getting customer complaints.'
- Mention it in your team meeting under customer complaints
- Bring it up in his performance review four months later
- Say 'I've just received two customer complaints. Can we talk about it?'

The first is a common but ill thought-out response which may feel aggressive to the other person and is too unspecific. The second is too public and the third is too late.

The effect of poor individual performance can damage the whole team, particularly if left unchecked. So, as in the last example, be specific and raise the issue in a factual, non-threatening way. Go through these steps:
1. First check you are being realistic in your expectations.
2. Clarify with the individual what is expected of them and ensure that there are no misunderstandings.
3. Identify the cause of the problem, which may be, for example:
   - Lack of knowledge/training
   - Personal problems
   - Working conditions, problems in the teams
   - Work organisation and work flow.

You are then able to set improvement goals. If these fail after warnings, then transfer or dismissal should follow. The short term disruption this will cause will pay off long term. Consult a personnel specialist to ensure you are following correct personnel procedures which are good practice and within the law.

The over performer
One of your team provides an excellent level of service to customers. As a consequence customers prefer to deal with this team member rather than other people in your team. She has well exceeded the objectives you set her last year. What do you do?

When the performance of an employee well exceeds the objectives there are a number of questions you should ask:
- Were the objectives set too low?
- Was the performance due to special circumstances?
- Is the person just very good?
- How can you develop this person?
- What extra training does this person need?

The aim should be to encourage their further development, to make good use of the employee's strengths, and avoid the risk of boredom setting in through lack of stretching tasks.

The experienced team member
There may be occasions when you have to review the performance of a member of staff who has been with the organisation for some time and who is very experienced but is unlikely to progress beyond their current level. This person may be a valuable source of information on longer-established clients. If you have a person like this in your team:
- Respect their experience but do not let this become a barrier to change
- Be open and honest about their career prospects
- Do not make assumptions about their motivation or prejudge their ability to enlarge their knowledge
- Use their experience in setting objectives and in solving problems jointly
- Accept that this person may have limited training and development needs through courses but still needs updating
- Encourage this person to be a mentor for less experienced employees.

The silent team member
There may be occasions when a member of staff is silent during a performance review and you have difficulty getting them to open up. Perhaps they have not understood the purpose of the review, or have not had an opportunity to prepare.

Alternatively they may feel that they have not been given an opportunity to express their thoughts and opinions or that their views are not valued. If this is the case:
- Be supportive – involve the employee in discussion and joint problem solving.

- Be equal, not superior. Ask for and listen to the employee's opinion. Be enthusiastic and receptive to new ideas.

REWARD AND INCENTIVE METHODS

Many managers advocate that pay should have a link to performance to provide motivation and feedback. The extent of this will differ from job to job and from company to company. The introduction of incentive methods can help you achieve better results. But to be effective you should ensure individuals can influence the desired outcome and that the results are measurable. You should consider:
- Who – individual or team
- What – money or a token
- Where – which locality
- When – monthly, quarterly, annually
- Why – what are you supporting?

Below are some of the methods.
1. *Payment for achievement of objectives.* This can have a powerful impact on getting target tasks achieved, though you need to take care that other, non-targeted areas do not suffer.
2. *Employee good performance awards* can lead to definite improvements if the culture is right. However, such schemes need to have clear and fair selection criteria if they are not to demotivate lots of others who wonder why they have not been chosen.
3. *Payment for suggestions.* Suggestions schemes can work well, though they may 'run out of steam' after a while. To work successfully there needs to be an easy method to send suggestions and they need to have a fast turnaround.
4. *Non-monetary rewards*, from a thank-you letter, to a meal out, can be beneficial motivators.

Link rewards to customer satisfaction

Both monetary and non-monetary rewards can be linked to the attainment of customer satisfaction targets. In our experience this is a powerful means of reinforcing the importance of customer satisfaction throughout the organisation.

Rewards can be made when teams reach improvement targets or for specific achievements such as speed of telephone response or friendliness and courtesy with customers. Such rewards can be made to both teams and individuals. Importantly, they must be seen by those involved to be relevant and fair.

Linking rewards to customer satisfaction targets is a powerful means to emphasize customer satisfaction.

Make certain too that the target level of customer service is not attained at the expense of other aspects of the service. For example, the improvement of overall telephone response is a more customer-orientated achievement than the speed of answering the phone. In the latter case the customer's call may be answered quickly, but the customer may be kept holding on the 'phone and may not be transferred efficiently.

SUMMARY

- Good performance management provides direct benefits to customers through a rigorous focused approach to achievement of goals.
- A manager can create a high-performing team and develop and motivate staff by:
  - establishing roles and key responsibilities
  - setting clear, measurable and realistic objectives
  - monitoring how well these are achieved.
- To ensure optimum team performance a manager needs the skills and knowledge to:
  - know what motivates his or her staff
  - provide regular feedback
  - review performance and set new objectives
  - decide on the most appropriate rewards and incentives.

EXERCISES

1. Decide the key result areas for your job and put them in writing. Discuss these with your whole team. Then set key result areas for the rest of your team by joint discussion. Objectives can be set for specific tasks.
2. Consider the link between motivation and rewards for you and your team:
   - What motivates you and what rewards do you value?
   - What motivates your people?
   - What rewards do your people value?
   - What can you deliver to reward and motivate your team?

   Then draw up a plan on how you can demonstrate to every member of your team that:
   - effort will lead to good performance, and
   - they will get rewarded for that.
3. Re-examine the last performance review you carried out. What was the effect on the individual's performance and motivation after that review? Looking back on how you handled the appraisal, did real two-way communication occur? Did you record the discussion and set clear objectives which you followed up? Consider asking the individual for candid feedback on how you conducted the review and how you can improve.

4. Review how you have managed the performance of your team over the last three months. What examples can you identify of ways you have helped to build a motivating climate by:
   - providing clarity of direction
   - making all individuals feel valued
   - providing scope for development
   - recognising achievements
   - providing challenge.
5. Ask your members of staff what they feel they have accomplished in the past month. Are there any changes they would like to see to help them perform better? Do they have any skills or aptitudes which are not being used? What areas of training do they feel would be beneficial to them?

◀ CHAPTER 12 ▶

TRAINING AND DEVELOPMENT

This chapter takes you through these topics:
- What your responsibility is for training and development
- Why they are important
- What options are open to you for developing your people
- When coaching is useful
- How you can create the optimum conditions for learning.

Training and development are high on the list of a manager's responsibilities. It is important to the manager in service situations because of the need constantly to keep up standards. Training and development are the primary vehicles for achieving this.

New employees need training to introduce them into the organisation. Existing employees need training, too, particularly as the pace of technological and market changes is so rapid today. Yesterday's standards are simply not good enough as the competition gets better. Employees also have come to expect training and development to support their career development and so that they can do a good job.

Employees today expect training and development, and they need it to keep pace with rapid technological and market changes.

There are three types of training and development which people working in a customer service environment require. These address:
- Knowledge
- Skills
- Attitudes.

Team members' knowledge needs to be developed or refreshed so that they can understand and explain the products and services the organisation provides. Specific skill training, such as keyboard skills and time management skills, is needed in many customer service organisations. Attitude, however, is the key to excellent customer service and this shows itself in areas such as willingness to help, concern for the customer and taking responsibility for problems.

SOME OBJECTIONS TO TRAINING

'I did my training when I was younger'
Training is a continuous process – no-one should ever stop learning otherwise the world will leave them behind.

'It's everyone for themselves round here. I'm not nannying my staff'
This is a charter to do nothing, so mistakes may continue and opportunities to develop be missed. You do not have to watch over someone continually to help them develop.

'It's expensive and disruptive'
There are costs involved, but also benefits. All training has to be a sensible balance between the two; you are making an important investment decision.

'If I train them too well, they will leave'
Of course you run this risk. But the more competent your people, the more satisfactory will be team performance. If you demonstrate you are giving something of benefit to individuals, they are more likely to feel positive and committed to the organisation. People expect to be developed. If you do not train them they may leave because the company is failing to meet their needs.

'It's when you can't do the job that you need to be trained up'
Many people see training as a one-off process designed to address a specific problem. This sometimes leads to people seeing training as being separate from work and the trainer as an expert to cure all ills. Training and development should, however, be a continuous process closely related to work issues. No one is ever 'fully trained' or an 'expert' and knowledge, skills and attitudes must be developed and enlarged as time progresses.

'It's not *my* job. I'm too busy!'
You cannot abdicate the manager's responsibility for staff development or minimise its importance. Good leadership in providing training will be reflected in competent, independent staff. Outside organisations or other departments can only support you, not take this responsibility away from you. So plan time to train and develop your people. Through your example you will demonstrate the importance of learning for job performance. In this way you will help people to link training back to their jobs and build success

through your confidence and the encouragement you give for people to learn new things and reach higher standards.

The questionnaire in Table 12.1 seeks to give you an assessment of how you see training and development in relation to your management task.

Table 12.1 *Training and development questionnaire*

Answer on a scale of 1 to 5, 1 where you strongly *disagree* with the statement and 5 where you strongly *agree*. Answer 2 if you disagree with the statement, 4 if you agree. Answer 3 if you neither agree nor disagree with the statement.

1.	Customers increasingly demand well-trained and well developed staff	1	2	3	4	5
2.	I closely match training and development to the needs of the business	1	2	3	4	5
3.	I set out a training and development plan for my people for 12 months ahead and review it regularly	1	2	3	4	5
4.	My staff know that training and development is important in our team	1	2	3	4	5
5.	I deploy a variety of training and development methods not just courses	1	2	3	4	5
6.	I make use of the development opportunities offered in projects, secondments and day-to-day tasks	1	2	3	4	5
7.	I see training as a method of improving productivity and changing behaviour	1	2	3	4	5
8.	I regularly review the development needs and career aspirations of my people	1	2	3	4	5
9.	I set development objectives and evaluate them	1	2	3	4	5
10.	Training is useful in creating the customer values and attitudes I wish to promote	1	2	3	4	5
11.	I believe coaching is one of the most valuable methods of learning	1	2	3	4	5
12.	I have a good understanding of how people learn best	1	2	3	4	5
13.	I give my staff at least five days' training each per year	1	2	3	4	5

Scoring

50–65: You understand and apply the benefits of training and development.

21–49: You have a reasonable grasp of training and development approaches. You could usefully learn more.

13–20: You could benefit from a wider view of the application of training and development to the business.

ENCOURAGING SELF-DEVELOPMENT

Increasingly companies are promoting self-development rather than a cradle-to-grave nurturing approach where the company takes care of your development for you. To create the right climate, give people the chance to use their talents fully. Talk to them about their aspirations and how the company can meet these. This is probably best done as part of a performance appraisal. Alternatively ask your team to identify their own development needs. You can also encourage the team to undertake its own training using the skills and knowledge from within the group or using the team leader or other team members as coaches.

Encourage the practice of internal promotion and development. It is tempting to try to keep talented employees in your team, but in the long run the company will benefit from retaining the employee in another area. Equally you will benefit from publicising internally opportunities to join your team.

Much of customer service revolves around the team. The team helps identify development needs and coaches from the resources within that team.

INDUCTION TRAINING

Even the best new starters need time to tune in to an organisation, to understand what is expected of them, who's who and who does what. Induction training aims to help new employees to settle in quickly and perform well, with the minimum delay. It should provide:
- An overall company perspective – its history and its products and services
- An understanding of the organisation's structure
- Rules, both written and unwritten, and expectations
- Health and safety procedures
- A knowledge of the location and its facilities
- A knowledge of customers and their expectations.

Some of this information needs to be put over as soon as an employee arrives, some can be done over the next few weeks and months. Develop a checklist of topics a newcomer needs to know. Sort all the details out before the new employee arrives, including any training plans, to give a good first impression.

THE NEED FOR A SYSTEMATIC APPROACH

Imagine you are the manager of a busy customer service environment. You receive several complaints from customers concerning the poor response of two of your team members on the 'phone. Later the same day another of your team members comes to you in tears as she feels she cannot cope with difficult customer situations and does not have your support. The previous week your team leader had said that there was dissatisfaction because staff did not feel their career development was being considered: a new recruit had just been appointed rather than there being promotion from within. What is going on here?

These are symptoms of lack of planning and analysis of training needs. The manager is responding to each crisis and problem in a piecemeal way and the business is suffering. What you would need to do in this situation is to take a systematic look at the needs of your business and your customers and see how these match up to the skills and attitudes of your staff. This would enable you to plan training and development to head off problems and make the most of the capabilities and ambitions of your staff.

A departmental training plan can help you tackle problems at source rather than responding to crises piecemeal.

It is therefore a good idea to go through the discipline of completing a training needs analysis and then a training and development plan for your department to gain a perspective on what training and development is needed.

This process starts off by asking: where do I want each of my team to be in order to reach my team goals? Where are they now? The more precise you can be the better, since you can assess the performance gap and make more accurate plans about what to do. You should aim to draw up a team training plan as shown in Table 12.2, based on an analysis of each person's training needs, after answering these questions:

- What is the business objective?
- Where are we now?
- Where is the gap?
- Is there a training solution?

Table 12.2 *Sample format for a training plan*

Who is involved	Training need	Suggested training to meet the need	When it should happen	Likely costs
Example				
All admin. staff	Improvement in department's telephone skills	One day telephone skills workshop	April 5th	£600

You will obviously need to be selective about what you can implement, so a good understanding of your priorities is vital. You should involve your staff in this process.

Ensure that the objectives of the training are clear. This means constructing a simple, precise statement of the standard of performance or behaviour expected at the end of the training: what do I need this person to know and do differently? What will be the evidence in their performance? The outcome of specifying development objectives is that you have a set of measures against which you can evaluate the training once this has taken place.

Here is an example of a training objective. By the end of the workshop participants will be able to:
- Answer the phone in a customer-friendly manner
- Handle customer queries in a concise and effective way
- Deal effectively with customer requests.

You should keep a record of training and development as part of a training and development plan since it will enable you to compare achievements against original expectations and give you access to a useful databank. Some companies are encouraging individuals to take more responsibility for their own learning by suggesting they keep a personal training and development plan and record. This is a simple diary of training and development with a record of what has been learnt against agreed plans. It encourages insight and understanding into oneself as well as personal ownership and development.

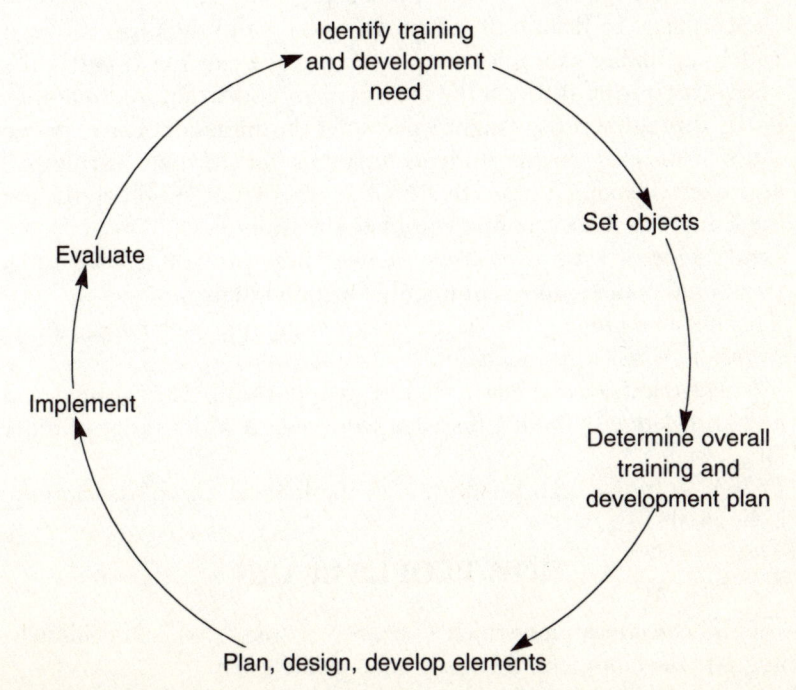

Figure 12.1 *A planned training and development cycle*

Whoever keeps this plan, you, as a manager, have a responsibility to ensure each individual has a written plan which provides information about what has been achieved, what training and development is needed and who can do what.

Figure 12.1 shows the training cycle from identification through to implementation.

TRAINING AND DEVELOPMENT OPTIONS

External courses are not the only answer – there is a wide range of training options.

What are the training and development options open to you? Many people immediately think of training courses, but there is a wide range of other choices, as follows.

- *Coaching.* This is the personal help you give your staff on the job to develop their skills to improve their ability to do the job. Its focus is very much on immediate results.
- *Visits or short secondments.* This is getting an insider understanding of a particular department or company. It is useful as a means to build up contacts as much as gaining specific knowledge.
- *Guided reading, videos, computer based learning.* This can impart knowledge at a time to suit the learner. It is particularly useful if backed up by discussion and review with the manager.
- *Open learning.* In Britain the Open University and the Open College are widely available examples of open learning. Learning is partly undertaken by yourself through the use of videos and structured reading and partly through written assignments under the guidance of an experienced tutor who may bring students together for further learning. This approach is flexible but needs a high degree of motivation on the part of the learner to persevere and complete the training.
- *Local colleges, evening courses/day release.* These provide a wide range of vocational courses, most commonly for individuals.
- *Trial and error learning.* This is the sink or swim approach which, although common, is risky and wasteful.
- *Job enlargement or cross training.* This is an opportunity to acquire new skills and knowledge by taking on extra work over a wider range of different jobs.
- *Projects.* A project can be given with the specific aim of developing the individual.

HOW PEOPLE LEARN

One of the considerations which you need to make when deciding your training and development options is how people learn.

A commonly held belief is that we only learn through experience. An inscription in ancient Greece read, 'Experience teaches'. There is also an old saying which goes:

 I read, I forget
 I see, I understand
 I do, I remember.

Yet to be successful, training and development should offer more than learning by doing. To make the most of a learning opportunity, people need to think about what they have learnt, why it has been successful or not and what to do differently next time.

We know from observation that different people are most comfortable when they are learning in preferred ways. Peter Honey says that there are four learning styles which can be used to characterise different learning preferences. People use all four styles but gravitate by choice to one or two of them. If we divide people into four types we can assess their corresponding preferred methods of learning.

1. *Action orientated.* These people learn primarily by doing. They enjoy the here-and-now of immediate experiences. Their motto is 'have a go'.
2. *Observers.* These people tend to stand back and reflect on experiences and observe them from many difference perspectives. In a training course they will want to ask 'can I review my video again?'
3. *Practitioners.* Practitioners are keen on ideas and eager to see if they work in practice. They need to ask 'what relevance is this?'
4. *Conceptualisers.* These people adapt and integrate observations into logical theories. They are not happy until they can see a pattern, a framework to help them understand. Their first response to a new situation will be 'Is there a book on this?'

These different ways of approaching learning are illustrated as a cycle in Figure 12.2. To achieve maximum effectiveness, training and development should encourage participants to learn by moving right round the cycle of learning. In this way learning is likely to stick and lead to permanent changes and improved performance.

People learn in different ways but should be encouraged to explore all approaches.

People learn best when they are motivated to learn and can see a definite benefit in doing so, particularly by applying the learning to their jobs quite quickly.

COACHING

Coaching is the ongoing personal help a manager gives to improve performance. This is probably the most effective form of learning. It puts the power and responsibility for development where it belongs, with the manager guiding and encouraging his or her staff as they carry out their jobs. Managers

120 LEADING YOUR TEAM RESOURCEFULLY

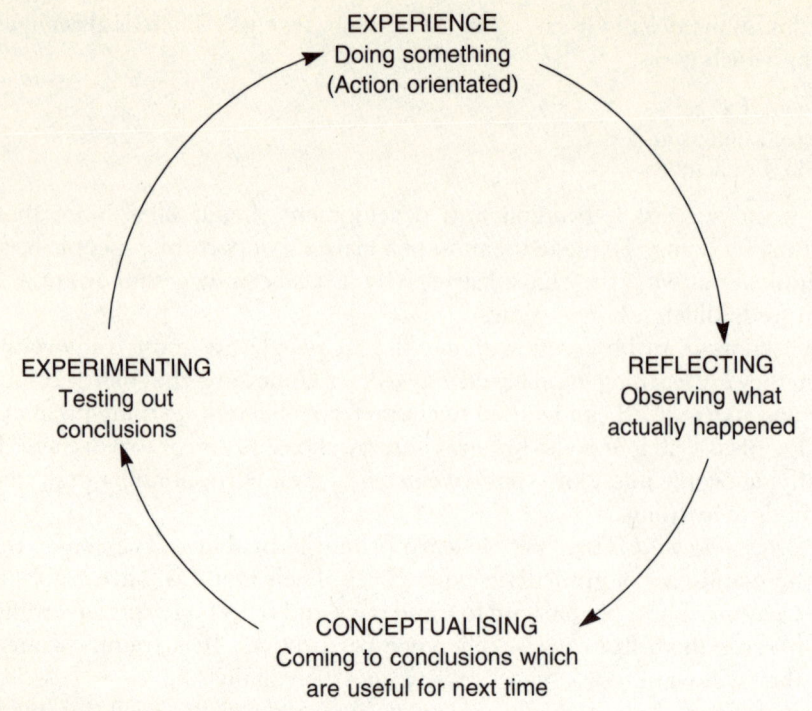

```
                    EXPERIENCE
                   Doing something
                  (Action orientated)



 EXPERIMENTING                            REFLECTING
   Testing out                          Observing what
   conclusions                         actually happened



                   CONCEPTUALISING
                Coming to conclusions which
                  are useful for next time
```

Figure 12.2 *A cycle of learning*

do this anyway; they often have to coach to get a job done. But do they do it well? What makes a good coaching relationship?

What makes for coaching success?
- Recognising coaching opportunities. Many development possibilities go by unnoticed in the heat of the moment. A good coach is always alert to possibilities to develop staff through assigning tasks which need to be done but have development possibilities if given to the right person.
- The quality of the relationship with your people and the management style you adopt. Coaching works best when the coach shows a willingness to listen and sometimes to accept critical feedback.
- The coach is supportive and encouraging, which reinforces new learning. Criticism is used sparingly and never in front of other people.
- Staff are involved in setting learning objectives and plans to carry them out. This is likely to lead to much higher commitment: coaching will succeed where staff can work out their own best way.
- The objectives are clear and the task is stretching, achievable and worth while.
- The coach is enthusiastic and displays good coaching skills – skilled

coaches are good communicators, patient and prepared to listen, and they are available if needed.
- The coach keeps a measure of control appropriate to the individual. They do not stand over the person nor do they abdicate responsibility, but they are accessible, they follow through and they give feedback to maintain progress.
- The individual receiving coaching is clear how to do the job and can see progress being made against well-defined standards and measures of success.
- There is no undue pressure, such as time deadlines or the threat of the consequences of failure.

Six steps in coaching

There are various steps you should follow in all coaching situations. However, the amount of your direct involvement, as a coach, will vary according to the experience level of the person being coached.

Where individuals have little or no knowledge of a procedure or task, the degree of coaching which they require will be greater than someone who has some skill but still needs to develop specific aspects of their job. The more experience and knowledge, the greater the independence you should offer. In either case, here are the steps in coaching an individual:

1. Clarify the problem or opportunity. Let the individual think it through fully with your help.
2. Set objectives with the individual and jointly agree the method of approaching the task. Be flexible about what this should be. Strike a balance between getting the best possible result and letting the employee come to their own conclusions.
3. Take one step at a time. Do not overload the individual all at once. Check understanding at each stage.
4. Allow enough time to make the task a success.
5. Provide feedback and review at regular intervals. Be specific. Praise good performance. Go easy on criticism.
6. Review final outcome against initial objectives.

These steps are summarised in Table 12.3.

Use a coaching plan to help you work out how you will conduct your coaching. This plan should outline:
- Objectives of coaching
- Stages
- Methods to be undertaken
- Timing
- How progress will be reviewed
- How you will know when the coaching has reached its objectives.

Table 12.4 is an example of a coaching plan.

Table 12.3 *Stages in the coaching process*

	Coaching project outline	**Project plan**	**Implementation**	**Completion**
Coach's actions	Clarifies and agrees objectives, standards, timescales	Discusses and agrees development plan	Reviews, encourages, assists only where appropriate. Gives feedback at progress meetings	Final task review. New development objectives set
Actions by person being coached	Inputs their views on what their objectives should be; what they feel is practicable, achievable; what help they will need	Jointly agrees plan	Seeks feedback, clarification. Asks for help where necessary	Receives feedback, takes part in objective setting for next plan

Table 12.4 *Sample coaching plan*

1. Objectives of coaching	2. Steps required	3. Method	Timing	Review
To develop Alison's ability in desktop publishing	1. Explain principles of system and provide opportunity to practice	1. John to demonstrate system	2/10	
	2. Set specific task to undertake on system	2b. Alison to use demonstration learning disk		
		2. Sarah to explain presentation requirements	9/10	
	3. Monitor and review task	3. Sarah to review work	16/10	16/10

PROJECTS

Projects provide a good opportunity for coaching and development. Consider the following for maximum learning benefit:
1. Set clear objectives.

2. Ensure the project is relevant and worthwhile.
3. Provide sufficient authority and resources to make it a success. Clear any obstacles and communicate to others in the organisation before you start.
4. Be seen to make good use of the project's results.

TRAINING COURSES

Training courses can be very useful, especially if linked to training on the job. Ensure course objectives fully meet the needs of the employee and hold a pre-course meeting to agree personal goals. Make sure also that the style of the course – participative, action orientated through to lecture or formal briefing – is suitable for the level of knowledge and learning style of the participant.

On return to work, review with the individual how far the course met the goals set, looking particularly to help implement lasting changes.

Running training courses

Many line managers believe that training courses should only be run by training specialists. However, with careful planning you can do a lot yourself without the time or expense of others. This has the advantage, if you make a success of it, of enhancing your credibility with your team. You also have a head-start on external trainers – you are already likely to have the confidence of your people.

Managers are well placed to run training courses for their own staff.

Tips for running training courses
- Prepare thoroughly – your overall objectives, and session-by-session objectives. To set learning objectives ask yourself 'What do I expect the individuals to know or do differently?'
- Plan your time accurately – ensure that you leave sufficient time for discussion, questions and practical exercises.
- Make the group size manageable – too big and people cannot participate, too small and it can lack energy. Ensure there are not widely different abilities.
- Check the size, shape, temperature and layout of the room.
- Create a consciously friendly atmosphere and help people to relax and enjoy the training.
- Start on a high note to gain attention.
- Watch you do not dominate the session by doing too much talking. Involve everyone as much as you can.
- Build in frequent opportunities for reinforcing the learning through practice or learning exercises. Recap periodically so that people have a chance to take stock of what they have learnt.
- Check that you are going at the right speed for the group to avoid boring

- people or alternatively losing them as they fail to keep up with you.
- Summarise at the end.

If you still feel unsure about running training courses, a trainer could help you by training with you and coaching you until you feel more comfortable.

DISCUSSIONS

Managers who train their staff need to be effective presenters (see Chapter 8 for some useful tips on presentation). A further skill which is important in training is that of leading a discussion. Here, the role of the manager is to:
- Prepare a framework for the discussion
- Guide and control the discussion
- Involve everyone
- Make good use of questioning to gain opinions
- Listen
- Summarise.

EVALUATING AND FOLLOWING UP TRAINING AND DEVELOPMENT

Many people believe that once training or coaching has taken place the training process is complete. However, the real learning takes place when skills are transferred to the workplace. It is important therefore to hold a development review meeting with a course member when he or she has returned to work. This ensures that the effectiveness of the training is evaluated against the objectives that have been set for it and an action plan is agreed to put the learning into practice. Managers should monitor the progress of their staff and provide support and encouragement as they try out new skills and methods.

Managers also have a vital role to play in reinforcing the training message by their example. They should also regularly review the performance of their staff and identify future training needs.

SUMMARY

- Training and development is particularly important to managers in customer service situations because of the need constantly to keep up standards.
- Managers should take the following steps to train and develop their staff:
  - Identify training and development needs and devise a training and development plan which is periodically updated

- Set specific objectives for any training and development
- Decide the most appropriate training and development method: do not automatically choose a course
- Evaluate the effectiveness of training and development
- Monitor and review the performance of staff to set new development objectives.
* Make the most of coaching. If you do everyone will benefit: you in the time saved through making staff more autonomous, the employee in developing their confidence and skills.

EXERCISES

1. Review the specific training and development needs of your staff in consultation with them. Draw up a plan itemising the training and development required, when it will take place, the method chosen and the action required to progress this. Record also when the effectiveness of the training will be reviewed.
2. Consider the training and development methods you are currently adopting within your company. Review how these could be broadened and improved.
3. Practise role playing with a colleague in a one-to-one coaching situation. Check your strengths in three major areas – that you demonstrate careful listening, that you are communicating clearly, and that you have tested the other person's understanding of what you have said.
4. Offer to contribute your knowledge of customers and what they need to other groups in the company as part of any ongoing training.

◀ CHAPTER 13 ▶

THE INTERNAL CUSTOMER

The service an organisation provides is only as good as the way people work together within it. In this chapter, we consider team working across departments, through exploring the concept of the internal customer. We will describe:
- What internal customers are
- What standards you should set in the treatment you give them
- How you the ultimate customer can benefit by better cooperation inside the organisation.

WHAT IS AN INTERNAL CUSTOMER?

Everyone in an organisation serves the customer, but some teams are doing this primarily by serving other departments. They have internal customers. This process can sometimes fall down because each department puts emphasis on their own priorities:
- The purchasing department buys cheaply, but quality is poor and the customer returns product
- The production department seeks long production runs and builds up excess stock which is a drain on the company's cash
- The warehousing department keeps stocks too low and customers have to wait for delivery
- Marketing fails to tell the service department of model changes and so customers wait weeks for new parts
- A credit controller puts a key customer on credit hold for a small amount at a time which could prejudice the negotiations for a big order

Are there such examples of inconsistencies and inadequate inter-departmental cooperation in your organisation? There almost certainly will be, so it is fruitful to examine how you can ensure that your department delivers a good service to the others.

WHY INTERNAL SERVICE QUALITY CAN BE POOR

All too frequently the quality of service which departments provide each other can be poor. What are the principal causes?

1. We have mentioned that departments put an emphasis on their own priorities. Often departments do not see themselves as having customers, especially those departments who do not directly interface with the external customer.
2. In many cases departments are not aware of the roles and responsibilities of other parts of the organisation. There can be a general lack of understanding of who does what and little contact between different departments.
3. Sometimes departments fail to recognise the link between the service they provide and the overall service which the organisation delivers. They do not have an overview of the contribution they make to customer service.
4. Often there can be a lack of awareness that customers are the most important asset an organisation has. This manifests itself in lack of responsibility for customer problems or a 'them and us' attitude between front line and support staff.

Each department needs to recognise the link between the quality of service they provide the rest of the organisation, and the quality of service which reaches the customer.

HOW TO PROVIDE A GOOD SERVICE TO THE INTERNAL CUSTOMER

The first and most important step is to gain the commitment of senior management to improving the way each department serves each other. In practice this means getting everyone involved in improving the service they give to their internal customers. Here are some suggestions which you can implement.

- Define who are your key internal customers. Get your people together and set out what the customers expect of you. Be specific: what delivery dates, what standards do they expect? Then rate on a scale 1 to 10, how effective you are at delivering the service. When you have done this, check it out with these departments and agree targets for improvement.
- Consider conducting an internal customer feedback survey on a similar basis to an external customer survey. Table 13.1 is an example. This needs to be fully explained to your team beforehand so that they will not feel too defensive and so that they see the benefits, which are, particularly, improved understanding.

Consider conducting an internal customer feedback survey on a similar basis to an external customer survey.

128 LEADING YOUR TEAM RESOURCEFULLY

- Encourage the development and communication of company goals and values which everyone buys into. In this way everyone has a clear understanding of priorities that the customer comes first and their job is to help meet that goal.
- Readily give credit where it is due to other departments. If they have done a good job in helping your department, let them know through a thank you memo and personal thanks.

Do not spring too many surprises on other departments or you may not gain their cooperation when you really need it.

- Plan ahead your workload and anticipate where you need to involve other departments. Do not spring too many sudden surprises on them, so that at times when you do have a crisis or need to change your plans you can be assured that they will pull the stops out to help. Involvement of other departments gains their commitment, and is also a source of fresh ideas.
- Keep other departments informed – of new products, services, prices, new people, organisation changes, and so on. There is rarely a danger of over-communicating, but think carefully what information other departments need and how best to present that.
- Help everyone to be aware that customers' needs come first, through campaigns, newsletters and other promotional means. Give everyone the chance to know more about the customer and the products and services you are offering, otherwise they may not fully appreciate their contribution to meeting customer needs.
- Include on induction courses and other training programmes references to the prime importance of the customer at all times.
- Do not just criticise other departments. Work to overcome differences by jointly examining difficulties. Treat other departments with courtesy and respect – just as you would external customers.
- Your role as a manager is as a link-person with other departments. Agree expectations between your team and other departments. Ensure these expectations are realistic and then make sure they are met.
- Encourage your team to get to know the other parts of the organisation, and vice versa. For example, invite other departments to your communication meetings.

Arrange for members of your team to work in other departments for a short period as this can give them valuable insights and help them forge contacts.

- Arrange for members of your team to work in other departments for a short period. This can give staff contacts and valuable insights into what service they need to provide.
- Encourage secondments and job sharing between departments.
- Hold a social get-together with the departments to whom you supply a service. Foster both formal and informal communication links.
- Supply regular updates of who you are and who does what in your department so that your customers, internal and external, know who to contact. Make sure your telephone directory is up to date.

- Hold an open forum for your customers in other departments. Put on a display of the work that you do. Invite comment and questions from your customers.
- Set up cross-departmental service improvement teams to discuss how you can jointly improve the service you provide the external customer.

Table 13.1 *Example of an internal customer survey*

1. What standards of service do you expect from our department?
2. What is the most important element of the service we provide?
3. Rate how satisfied you are with the service we provide as a department on a scale of 1 to 10 where 1 = very poor, and 10 = excellent.

Your satisfaction (out of 10)

1. *Telephone*
   a. Promptness of answering the call
   b. Manner in which telephone answered
   c. Availability of person to whom you wish to speak
2. *Written correspondence*
   a. Speed of response to written requests
   b. Accuracy of response
   c. Helpfulness
   d. Clarity

SUMMARY

- The quality of service which reaches the external customer is often determined by the quality of service internal departments provide each other.
- Many organisations fail to work together in a cooperative and courteous manner. A programme to emphasise that departments have internal customers can produce benefits for the organisation.
- Each department should recognise who are their customers and establish their expectations and satisfaction with the level of service they currently provide.
- The means to do this include an internal customer survey, joint working parties and secondments, and cross training between departments.

- Improving information and understanding is one of the most critical areas in developing inter-departmental cooperation.

EXERCISES

1. Discuss with your department who are your customers and how well you are meeting their needs. Ask your internal customers for input: what wastes their time? what do you do which helps and hinders the achievement of their goals? What would be the most significant improvement they would like? Discuss what you can do to improve the service you provide and develop a plan of action.
2. Plot out who provides a service to you and to whom you provide a service. Discuss with your team where you are in the service chain within your organisation. Define improvements which can be made to exceed external customer expectations.
3. Audit your communication links with the rest of the organisation. How do your internal customers gain information about you? How accurate is it? What ways are there to promote your organisation internally? Do people outside your department hear enough of your successes? Do they only hear of failures?
4. Conduct a review of the effectiveness of your team against meeting internal and external customer needs. Look at:
   - role definitions
   - reward and performance measures
   - organisation structure.

   Does your organisation meet the needs of your customers? Has it got out of date?

◀ PART 3 ▶

MANAGING YOURSELF

◀ **CHAPTER 14** ▶

DEVELOPING YOURSELF

In this chapter we examine:
- Why self-awareness and personal development are important for a manager in a customer service environment
- How you can develop a greater self awareness
- What you can do to increase your self-awareness and development as a manager in a customer service environment.

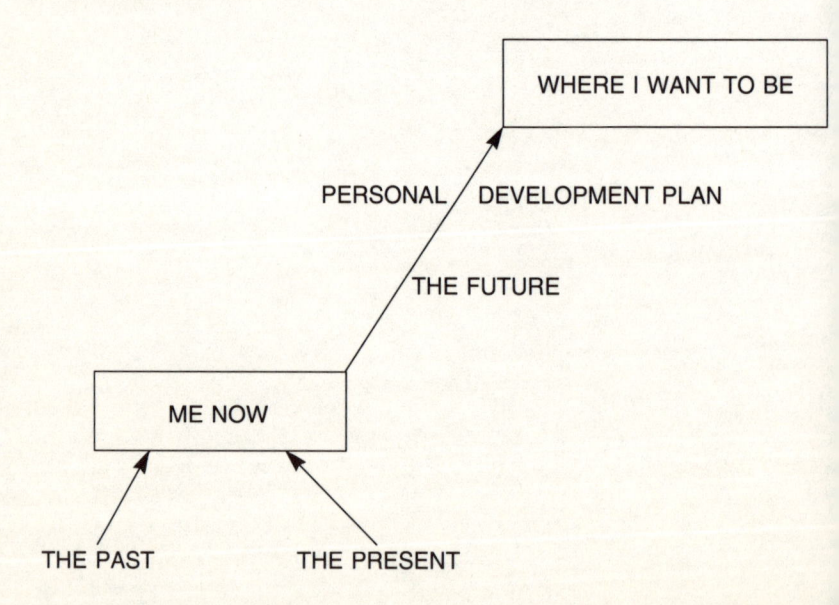

```
                              ┌──────────────────────┐
                              │ WHERE I WANT TO BE   │
                              └──────────────────────┘
                                        ↑
                         PERSONAL / DEVELOPMENT PLAN

                              THE FUTURE

              ┌──────────────┐
              │   ME NOW     │
              └──────────────┘
                ↑          ↑
           THE PAST    THE PRESENT
```

Figure 14.1 *Self-development*

WHAT ARE SELF-AWARENESS AND PERSONAL DEVELOPMENT AND WHY ARE THEY IMPORTANT?

Self-awareness and the ability to continue developing yourself are a recognition of your own strengths and weaknesses,- both in terms of your own perceptions of yourself and how other people perceive you. Self-knowledge is the first step in self-development – see Figure 14.1. Understanding yourself and a willingness to do better are important because in a busy customer service environment you need to be able to deal with customers, team members, your colleagues and your manager in a confident, positive and sensitive manner. You will achieve this more effectively if you are aware of your own capabilities and can draw on inner resources as the needs demand. In knowing your limitations you will be aware when you should ask for the support and assistance of others.

Understanding your own strengths and weaknesses is the first step in self-development.

A LOOK THROUGH YOUR WINDOW

The Johari window in Figure 14.2 is named after the first names of its inventors, Joseph Luft and Harry Ingham. It is a useful framework for exploring and extending your self-awareness. It uses two dimensions and two divisions of these dimensions to describe you – what is known by yourself, and what is unknown to you, and what is known by others and what is unknown to them. There are four windows which you and other people can look through. These windows can be big or small.

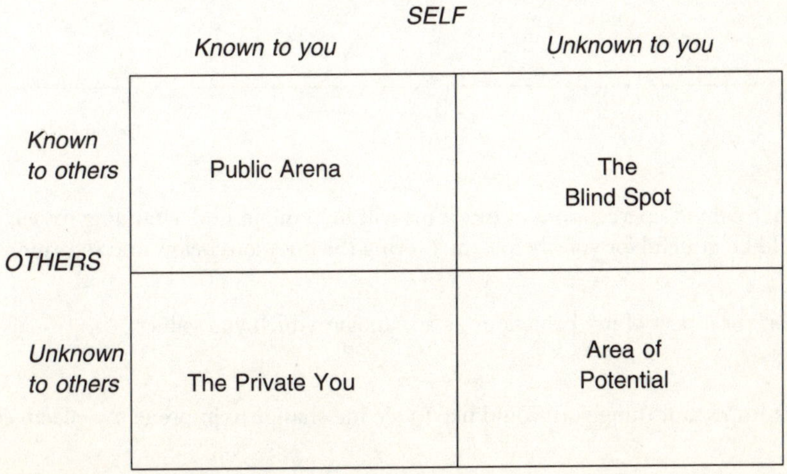

	SELF Known to you	SELF Unknown to you
OTHERS Known to others	Public Arena	The Blind Spot
OTHERS Unknown to others	The Private You	Area of Potential

Figure 14.2 *The Johari Window*

134 MANAGING YOURSELF

Feedback from colleagues illuminates the 'blind spot' we all have about ourselves.

Public arena
This is our public front, the one we show to customers and colleagues. How do you come across? Have you ever asked for any feedback? First impressions can be particularly important here.

The 'blind spot'
Sometimes other people will see you differently from the way you see yourself and you may be unaware of this; for example, what you see as speaking directly and in a straightforward manner, might come across to others as aggressive. Check how others see you – your boss and your colleagues can give you useful information here.

The private you
There are some things you naturally wish to keep to yourself, particularly in a work context. However, if you are too much of a closed book, other people may see you as unwelcoming or disapproving. Equally, being inappropriately open can unsettle a working relationship.

The area of potential
This is the area of unknown potential. The aim must be to increase your self-knowledge and reduce this hidden area.

GETTING FEEDBACK FROM OTHERS

The most effective way to find out how others see us is to ask them. Use the form in Table 14.1 to get some thoughtful feedback from other people. It is

Table 14.1 *Feedback form*

TO (NAME):

I am collecting data on other people's perceptions of me. This will help me in understanding myself and where I can develop. I would be grateful for your help in answering the questions below and returning this form to me.

1. What is the most important aspect of my behaviour as a manager which you value?

2. What is the single most important thing you would like to see me change to improve my effectiveness as a manager?

likely to be helpful to you to hear from critics as well as allies. You may well discover some nice surprises and perhaps some hurtful observations. You will need to exercise judgement on the validity of what is being given to you as feedback. Be prepared to ask for clarification and examples where this would help you.

It is likely to be helpful to hear from critics as well as allies.

HOW OK ARE YOU?

How we respect and value ourselves and other people can have a significant impact on how we behave towards customers and colleagues and how we feel about them.

Feeling OK or good about yourself helps you to be confident and flexible in customer contact. Feeling not OK leads you to look on the dark side and to emphasise negative feelings in yourself. Feeling OK about other people helps you to see the good in people. Feeling not OK about other people sees them as problems.

Originally developed by Thomas Harris, this 'OK–not OK' model about our attitudes to ourselves and others, helps us to construct a model of approach and behaviour. Consider the following typical ways of thinking about ourselves and others. Each of us tends to operate in one predominant area.

I'm not OK, you're OK
Self-confidence and self-esteem are very low here. These people will probably be sensitive to criticism and are likely to be resentful of other people. They may give in easily, using typical phrases such as 'Oh, that's typical of me' or 'I wish I could do that'. To customers they will come across as passive and lifeless.

I'm not OK, you're not OK
These people are doomed to fail – and it shows. Not only is their self-confidence low, but they are suspicious and cynical of other people.

Phrases that might be used by this person are 'What's the point', 'You never get anywhere'. To customers they will come over as depressed and unhelpful.

I'm OK, you're not OK
This is the aggressive approach. You feel perfectly good about yourself, but it is at the expense of others. You are quick to find fault or to blame and to judge others, slow to see the positive.

Typical phrases are: 'That's typical of you', 'Why don't you do something right for a change?', 'You've read the instructions wrongly'. Customers may well find these people supercilious and blaming.

I'm OK, you're OK

This is where you feel good about both yourself and other people. You come across as confident and helpful. This is based on well-founded sureness of your own strengths and the ability to see the good side in others.

Typical phrases might be 'I'm pleased I could help', 'Can I do this for you?', 'It's a lovely morning'. Customers will gravitate towards this person: the naturally smiling, helpful representative.

We can put this concept together into the framework shown in Figure 14.3.

```
                        I'm OK
                          |
                          |
                          |
    You're not OK ————————+———————— You're OK
                          |
                          |
                          |
                       I'm not OK
```

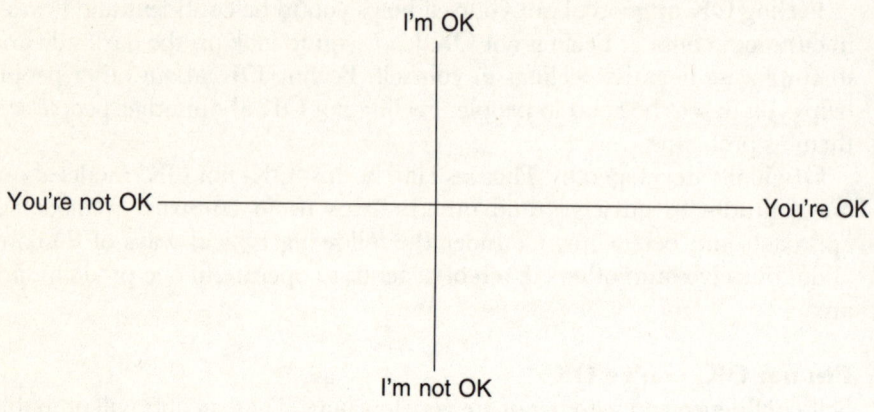

Figure 14.3 *The OK–not OK model*

Which of the four states most closely resembles you? Are there situations where you feel less confident than others and does this lead you to slip into a less desirable service approach? Try completing the following:

1. Situations where I feel OK about myself

2. Situations where I feel not OK about myself

3. Situations where I feel OK about others

4. Situations where I feel not OK about others

Now reflect back on your answers. What common threads are there a) when you feel good about yourself and others b) when you feel negative? Is there any way that you can increase the situations where you feel good and reduce the situations where you feel bad?

FEELING POSITIVE ABOUT YOURSELF AND OTHER PEOPLE

Look again at how you have completed the last exercise. How many occasions are there when you feel negative about yourself or other people? How do you think this has come across to customers?

Sometimes you may find it difficult to find positives in yourself or other people. Use this simple exercise to begin to see how every cloud has its silver lining.

List five attributes of yourself or someone you know well which you find negative or irritating.

1. ....
2. ....
3. ....
4. ....
5. ....

Now try and reframe these attributes so that you see the opposite, positive side of each of them. For example, you may think you are stubborn – the positive side of this is that you are therefore determined. You may think that someone is penny pinching – the positive side of this may be that they are good at managing their budget.

As a manager in a service situation, feeling positive and having a 'can do' approach is important. You are providing a leadership role in an environment where it may be very easy to see the dark side and become despondent. So reframe what you say into winning phrases:

- 'This could be an opportunity to try something new'
  rather than
  'It's hopeless – no one knows how to do it'
- 'We can be better than other companies'
  rather than
  'We're no worse than other companies'
- 'Let's tackle the problem'
  rather than
  'My bad luck again'

Everything has its positive and its negative side, so practise positive thinking.

- 'What can I learn from her?'
  rather than
  'I'm so jealous of her'
- 'I'm in charge of my own progression'
  rather than
  'Why doesn't someone give me a chance?'

So, remember to avoid the negative thinking and recognise and remind yourself of the things you are doing well.

SELF-AWARENESS AND DEVELOPMENT

Once you start gaining self-knowledge you will be able to develop more fully and appropriately, and the process is ongoing – see Figure 14.4.

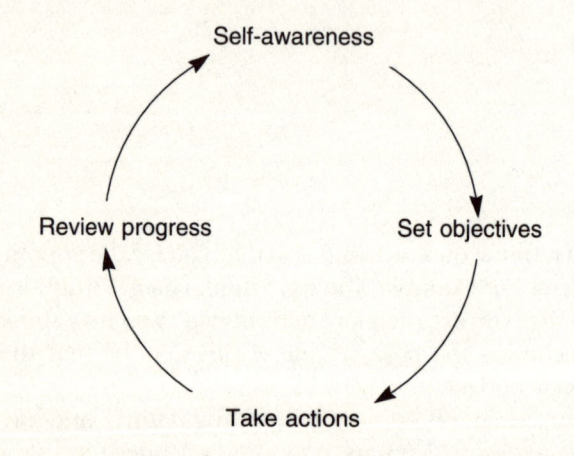

Figure 14.4   *The process of development through awareness*

Use the checklist in Table 14.2 to help you think about your skills in achieving good customer service. It is intended to help you identify personal development goals for yourself. For each item decide whether you need to do some work on it or if your performance is adequate or good. If there are items which you think are more important but which are not listed, add them – there is space provided below each section for you to do this.

Table 14.2 *Personal improvement checklist*

	Needs work	OK	Good

Self-development
Regularly take stock of my effectiveness
Invite feedback on my performance
Have clear personal goals
Identify self-development opportunities
Ask for help when I need it
Positive response to change

Personal management and organisational skills
Administration and paperwork
Time management
Delegation
Ensure appropriate and effective follow-up
Dealing with stress

Team management
Regularly review performance with my people
Take the lead in showing commitment to customers
Help staff to develop clear understanding of what is expected of them
Help team monitor its own performance
Communication: regular and two way?
Manage meetings
Cooperation with other departments

Performance management
Set and monitor agreed objectives and standards
Regularly hold performance reviews
Deal with difficult situations
Encourage active staff involvement
Give feedback – positive and negative

Handling people
1. General people skills
Listen carefully
Face up to awkward issues
Handling anger and conflict
Understanding of body language – mine and other people's
Assert myself where appropriate
Negotiate agreements which 'stick'

Table 14.2 *Personal improvement checklist* (contd)

	Needs work	OK	Good

2. Customer handling skills
Ensure I am prepared
Open in a friendly purposeful way
Close clearly and on a positive note
Use of questions
Listen effectively
Keeping control

Problem solving
Grasp the main issue
Seek ideas and opinions from others where appropriate
Listen to what others say
Set priorities
Be creative
Reach conclusions
Define clear actions

Other areas

SUMMARY

Self-awareness allows you to maximise your personal effectiveness. This means:

- Considering both the known and the lesser-known aspects of your personality, how you project yourself to other people and how honest you are with yourself
- Recognising that feeling OK about yourself and other people will help you deal positively with customer situations
- Turning potentially negative situations into positive ones
- Recognising your own strengths and weaknesses as a manager and drawing up an improvement plan for your personal development.

EXERCISES

1. Summarise what you have learnt about yourself in completing this chapter using Table 14.3.

Table 14.3 *SWOT analysis of yourself and current situation*

A SWOT analysis assesses **S**trengths, **W**eaknesses, **O**pportunities and **T**hreats. What are your main *strengths* and *weaknesses* – your personal capabilities, *opportunities* – external factors in your favour, *threats* – external barriers or obstacles which may hold you back, what could go wrong on the way to achieving your goals.

Strengths	Weaknesses
Opportunities	Threats

2. Now look at ways in which you can build on your strengths, overcome your weaknesses, take advantage of opportunities and minimise threats.
3. Set yourself some career goals. What do you want to be doing a year from now, three years from now, ten years on?
4. Develop a personal plan of action setting out the specific areas of improvement and development you wish to achieve.
5. Ask for feedback from other people on how well you are achieving your specific improvement goals.

◀ CHAPTER 15 ▶

TIME MANAGEMENT

This chapter considers:
- How you recognise the need for time management – in yourself and your team
- What you can do about time problems
- The aspects of time management particularly suitable in customer service.

COMMON OBJECTIONS TO APPLYING TIME MANAGEMENT TO CUSTOMER SERVICE

Time management is a key skill in implementing effective customer care. Yet many people find it difficult to manage time in a customer service environment.

Here are some plausible sounding objections which, if taken on board, effectively kill time management. Check out which ones, if any, particularly apply to you, but do not let these stop you in your tracks. Look for ways to overcome the problems.

'Customer problems are unpredictable. You can't plan when you never know what today will bring'
True, you need to be responsive, to be quick off the mark in dealing with customer issues. In practice, time management helps by juggling priorities and anticipating likely peaks or problems by planning ahead.

'You must never say no to customers'
While it is true that you should aim to achieve a high level of customer

TIME MANAGEMENT

satisfaction, saying yes blindly can lead you into a hopeless mess and promising things you cannot deliver.

'You never really know how long things take'
Practice in time planning gives you a reasonable track record of planning ahead. It is better to get that experience working within a planned framework even if not entirely accurate.

'Time management is too rigid for flexible-minded service structures'
Not if you stick to the principles of setting priorities and planning your time flexibly, and are not bound by rigid planning. A flexible time plan is better than no plan because it encourages anticipation and forces you to consider what is a priority. Be prepared to reorder what you have planned against new priorities and events and not schedule more than say half your day in advance.

'I'm not in charge of my time – other people are'
Everyone has some discretion or control over part of their job. Make the most of this. Try and gain more discretionary time; you may find you have more control than you realise.

'You can't get good staff, so you can't delegate'
Question how much you are holding back work from staff anxious to develop themselves and take on extra responsibility. Learn to trust your staff, anticipate ahead so that you have time to help them do a job with time to learn. Sometimes we have developed a self-fulfilling prophecy of low expectations that leads us to over-manage others. Consider letting go a bit more.

'I'm always in meetings'
Try and cut down the meetings and discipline yourself to make those you do attend shorter and more productive.

'You can spend all your day planning and writing lists'
Carefully thinking things through paves the way to a quicker, better result because it speeds up the final action process. You go up fewer blind alleys.

'I'm at the mercy of other people's poor time management'
Your good time management will help you to anticipate problems and take corrective action. You can negotiate your priorities more effectively from a position of strength if you are very clear what they are.

Time management is a key component of the provision of good customer service. It helps the manager and his or her staff in:
- Anticipating problems before they become crises
- Keeping a clear view of priorities for action
- Sticking to solving the important issues in the face of other distracting and diverting interruptions
- Juggling a wide range of issues and tasks at once
- Emphasising effectiveness not activity.

RECOGNISING BAD TIME HABITS

Here are some common symptoms of poor time management. Do any of these have a familiar ring to them?
- I feel I have an unbalanced workload
- Fire fighting and crisis response are the norm in my job
- Everything is a priority – I can't see the wood for the trees
- I'm doing too much and delegating too little.

If they do, your effectiveness in serving the customer has been reduced. Time management unlocks useful time and frees you from some pressures.

Time management unlocks useful time and releases pressure.

HOW TO MANAGE YOUR TIME BETTER

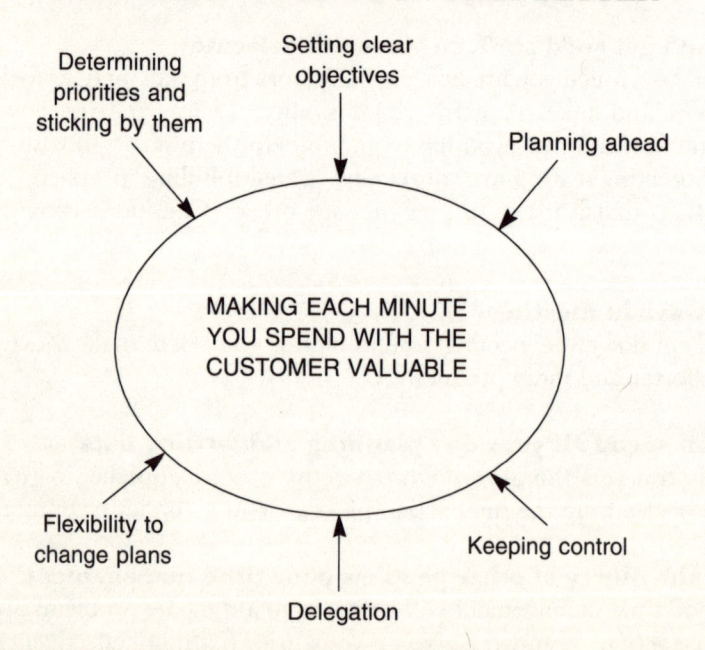

Figure 15.1 *Time management to serve your customer well*

TIME MANAGEMENT

Time management gives you better choice in how you use your time, through better planning and control. In this way you are more able to meet the real needs of the customer instead of wasting time and energy on unfruitful activities. Figure 15.1 illustrates this.

The first essential step in better time management is to establish how you should be spending your time – what your responsibilities, priorities and objectives are. Once you know what you should be doing you can then eliminate any unnecessary and inappropriate activities. As managers in a customer service environment it is quite clear where your priorities lie – with customer issues. So how much of your time is spent in non-productive work which is not serving the customer?

How much of your time is spent in non-productive work, not serving the customer?

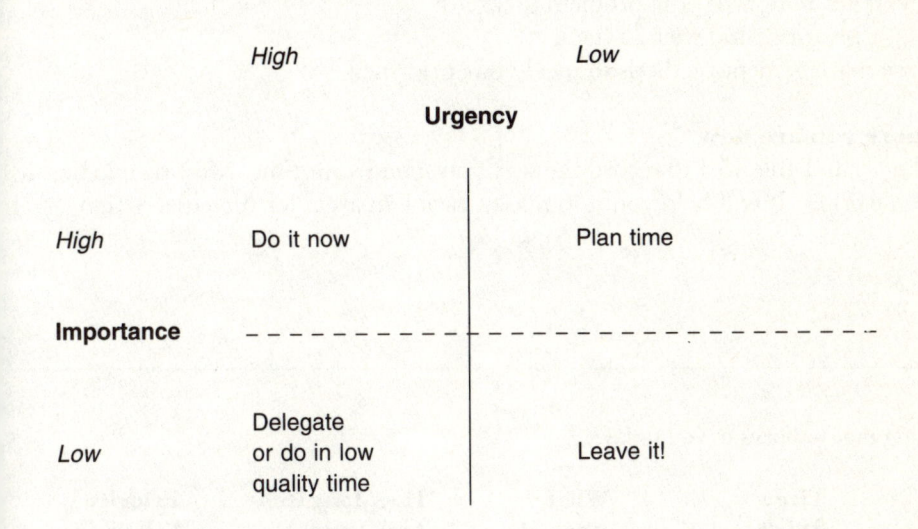

	High	Low
	Urgency	
High	Do it now	Plan time
Importance		
Low	Delegate or do in low quality time	Leave it!

Figure 15.2 *Prioritising work*

To help sort your way through the plethora of demands on your time, it is useful to prioritise your work into activity which takes account not just of urgency but importance too, as in Figure 15.2. Customer services are bedevilled by large amounts of interruptions, crises and fire fighting. So categorise your work into these areas:

1. Urgent and important work which needs to be done straight away
2. Important but not urgent work which should have second priority and be planned into your schedule; these are often long-term tasks
3. Not important but urgent work, usually smaller tasks which you should complete rapidly in 'low-quality time', for example when you might get interrupted, or work you can delegate

Work can be categorised into four levels of importance and urgency; doing this can help you decide *what* you do *when*.

4. Not important and not urgent tasks; this is activity which can wait to be completed or which you can complete in between other tasks, such as reading mailshots, returning unsolicited 'phone calls. These should be fourth on your list of priorities. Consider leaving them undone.

THREE-STEP APPROACH TO APPLYING A TIME MANAGEMENT STRATEGY TO GOOD SERVICE

Here is a stepped approach to managing your time more effectively and to applying these principles to your team:
1. Know where you are now, what the problem areas are
2. Understand your priorities and stick to them
3. Implement time management methods to meet your priorities.

Step 1: know where you are now
1. Keep a time log as in Table 15.1 to record the way you spend your time. Most people find it contains some surprises. It will help you to pinpoint problem areas for remedial action.

Table 15.1 *Time log*

Instructions:
Note down everything that happens to you today.

Time start	Time finish	What happened	How long it took (mins)	Priority A, B or C (A = high, C = low)
Example:				
9.45	10.15	Customer Meeting	30	A

TIME MANAGEMENT

2. At the end of the day, use Table 15.2 to analyse how much of your day was spent on priority tasks (As), how much on medium priority tasks (Bs), how much on low priority tasks (Cs).

Table 15.2 *Work analysis*

Task Priority	Minutes	% of your total working time
How much of your time was spent on each priority?		What percentage is this of the working period?
A		
B		
C		
Totals		100

3. Look back and review where your day went. Note aspects which you could:
   - shorten
   - eliminate
   - delegate.
4. Use Table 15.3 to pinpoint time wasters, those activities which waste your time and those of other people and which you can eliminate or drastically reduce to make you more effective.

Table 15.3 *Time waster analysis chart*

Time waster	Possible causes	Ways to overcome problems	Your improvement plan
Visitor after visitor	Inability to say 'no' Enjoys meeting people too much	Courteously put off drop-in visitors or reschedule their visits Filter callers	
Phone call after phone call	Busy job with a lot of contact with others Can't say 'I'll ring you back when I'm free' Over-long conversations	Time 'phone calls and analyse results Batch together return 'phone calls	
Always on the go	Liking of firefighting Lack of focus on achieving results Unrelaxed personality type Doing too much	Think before doing Focus on key results Learn relaxation techniques Delegate more	

Time waster	Possible causes	Ways to overcome problems	Your improvement plan
Crisis after crisis	Poor planning Unable to separate the urgent from the important	Review crises and causes Implement more effective planning Build in contingency time between fixed activities	
Work is one long meeting	Insufficient questioning of why meetings are being held Unclear objectives of meetings No agenda No clear actions and responsibilities for actions No control	Review meetings you attend Clarify objectives Issue agenda Assign actions Ask for feedback from meeting for areas to improve	
Mountains of paper	On too many circulation lists 'Just in case' information Lack of organisation Avoiding taking decisions	Come off mailing lists Sort into priorities Throw away rubbish Organise your workspace Set aside some quiet time for important tasks Handle each piece of paper as few times as possible	
Volume overload	Takes on too much Poor delegation Hesitates over decisions Inadequate grasp of priorities Unsystematic approach	Delegate more Identify priorities Don't procrastinate Start with the important things not the least important	

Step 2 understand your priorities and stick to them

1. Make sure you communicate clear messages concerning key priorities, values and objectives. This means you need to clarify these priorities with yourself first and regularly update this view. Remember the 80:20 rule in Figure 15.3. This says that we spend 80 per cent of our day producing perhaps only 20 per cent of importance. This seems to hold true whatever job we do in whatever organisation. Service organisations are particularly prone to this rule with lots of tasks, each seeming at first sight equally important. Most of our time is taken up with low impact tasks. We can increase effectiveness by spending more time on the 20 per cent of tasks which produce 80 per cent of the results.

```
           EFFORT    RESULTS
          ┌──────┐
          │ 80%  │  ┌──────┐
          │      │  │ 20%  │
          │      │ ↗│      │
          │      │ │├──────┤
          │      │╱ │      │
          ├──────┤╱ │ 80%  │
          │ 20%  │↗ │      │
          └──────┘  └──────┘
```

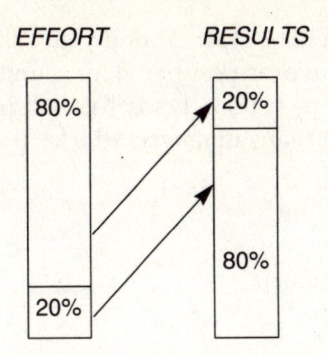

Figure 15.3 *The 80:20 rule: 80 per cent of effort produces 20 per cent results*

2. Put things first. Get on with the priorities straight away each day. Do not use valuable time to deal with the thousand and one low-priority tasks to get them out of the way – they will always take longer than you think.
   Remember to make best use of your peak energy time. Are you at your best in the morning or the afternoon? Use your peak energy time to complete those activities which are most difficult or where you need most concentration.
3. Assign a priority rating to customer issues. One method is a simple, A, B, C ranking, A being the most important, C the least. This ensures the greatest impact for the effort you put in.
4. Be decisive and do not always wait for that extra piece of information. You may be feeding time-consuming procrastination without producing noticeably better decisions.

Step 3: implement new methods

1. Get a grip on your paperwork. In a hectic service environment paperwork builds up very quickly and you can waste time finding papers, sorting through the muddle. To achieve order in your paperwork, make sure you have regular springcleans and organise your paper into appropriate categories which will work for you.
2. Implement a flexible planning system for your time usage. Break larger tasks down into smaller more manageable ones and put deadlines on each of them.
   Start the week by writing a list of your tasks, assigning priorities and then by planning ahead against expected workload. Do this in more detail each morning or last thing the night before to allow a 'brain dump' of ideas. Pick optimum times for the big tasks and key profit areas. As the day goes on, expect to reorder these priorities and timings against your priority ratings.
3. Guard against being interruption driven. It is common for most service staff to get a buzz from dealing with interruptions and crises but this 'action man' approach can take over. It can pay you to make time for important tasks by screening out interruptions. Divert the 'phone, tell colleagues to avoid interruptions for, say, the next hour, remove yourself physically to another place to work if necessary. Arrange cover for this time if required. More work requiring thinking time will get done more quickly in this way.

4. Delegate and use fully the resources of the people around you. Where appropriate, delegate as many activities outside your key tasks as possible. This sounds drastic advice to many customer service managers, but too many believe themselves indispensable and so never trust staff sufficiently to let go. You will hear many managers who keep a lot of work to themselves saying these sort of things :

>'My staff are just as overstretched as me'
>'It is quicker to do it myself'
>'You can't afford mistakes with customers'
>'I can't spare the time to train anyone'
>'It takes years to learn what I know'
>'You need first-hand knowledge to deal with customers'.

What they do not say is that they do not have confidence in their staff. They regularly undermine their staff by looking over their shoulders, finding fault or giving them unsatisfying, incomplete parts of a job. This is a vicious circle, since staff who fear mistakes, who have never been encouraged to take on new and challenging work and are not rewarded for doing so, will back off from responsibility.

Do not be tempted to cling on to too large a problem caseload and solve issues yourself. You may be the best person to fix the situation but is this making best use of time? What does this say about your trust in the capabilities of your staff?

Have confidence in your team's ability and learn to let go. To help you do this you should set out a delegation plan, as in Table 15.4, which identifies what you can relinquish and to whom. Agree this with the individuals. This will set out what is to be delegated, a target date and any development needed to make it work properly. Remember to consider individuals' development needs. Do not be too specific about how you expect the task to be achieved; leave this to the other person. Specify that the individual can come back to you if there is a problem.

Table 15.4 *Example of delegation plan*

Objective: To ensure Sally Jones takes over as team leader, help desk, while team leader is on holiday during August.

Tasks to be assigned	Development and training plan	Action	Date
Rota planning	1 day with team leader	SJ	June 23
Supervision of team	Supervisory development	RB	July 10/13
Red alert procedure	Briefing on procedure and case load by team leader	SM	July 25
Procedure for handling new service contracts	Company contracts course	Training	June 11
Workload handover	Sit in on weekly meetings dealing with current issues	SJ/SM	July 15 onwards

To delegate effectively:
- Sort out how much of your work only you can do then decide who could do the rest, either by virtue of their existing experience, or the development needs of your people
- Be clear about what is needed
- Explain what is to be done, why and by when
- Tell the person what authority they have and make this clear to other people
- Check progress at regular intervals, but do not interfere
- Provide support and encouragement – but resist the temptation to interfere.

5. Use a diary to support your time management. Most people use diaries only to record formal meetings and appointments, but they can become a total time planner, a means to plan ahead all the hours you work with other people and with yourself – in effect planning meetings with yourself. Many people find proprietary personal organisers valuable not only as a diary but to keep information together and give you a personal planning tool.

SUMMARY

- Good customer service requires disciplined time management through a three step approach:
    - know where you are now
    - stick to your priorities
    - implement new methods.
- Be clear about your objectives and the activities you need to undertake to achieve these.
- Plan how long it will take to perform these activities and tackle each one in sequence, though be flexible about time planning in a busy service environment.
- Focus on the important issues. Keep asking how what you are doing is best serving the customer.
- Identify time wasters and eliminate these.
- Delegate as many activities as possible outside your key tasks.
- Keep control of your time – do not let it control you.

EXERCISES

1. To make a start on new habits of time management, list the areas which you should improve upon, together with an action plan of what to do to get started and when. Set yourself monthly, weekly and daily objectives. Monitor these carefully.
2. List those people who need your time and those people whose time you need. Identify those people who take up too much of your time and those people who need to give you more of their time. Set up a one-to-one meeting with each person to discuss your respective priorities and expectations. Agree how to make better use of the time you spend together.
3. The first six weeks of implementing time management practices are crucial. Record the

improvements you make in your time management over the next two weeks and identify further areas for improvement for the following two weeks. Give yourself a well-deserved pat on the back for the progress you make. Do not get too downhearted by the occasional lack of progress in some areas.
4. Identify tasks which you can delegate to others and draw up a delegation plan covering each of your team.

◀ CHAPTER 16 ▶

MANAGING UNDER PRESSURE

This chapter considers how to recognise and deal with the pressures and stresses of a customer service environment. Specifically, it addresses:
- What stress is and how it differs from pressure
- How stress affects people in a customer service environment
- The causes of stress
- How you recognise stress in yourself and others
- What remedies you can apply
- Your responsibilities for the management of stress in your team

Stress and pressure management is particularly applicable to people who work in customer service environments because the job of many front-line staff in dealing with customers is very stressful. Invariably customers only contact you with complaints, queries or difficulties, sometimes with considerable ill-feelings. This may lead to relentless pressure which can build up. The effect of this is that customer service staff can feel tired, irritable and suffer ill-health. Worse, from the customer contact point of view, they may show some of this to the customer or simply not function well. This is not good for business and it certainly is not good for morale and long-term health and welfare.

Are the techniques of stress and pressure management capable of adaptation to the particular demands of customer service?

It is unlikely that the pressures can be altered, but the ability to cope with pressure can be enhanced. This comes about:
1. Through better recognition of what causes stress and how this varies from individual to individual
2. By knowing and understanding the symptoms of stress

It is unlikely that pressures can be altered, but the ability to cope with pressure can be enhanced.

154 MANAGING YOURSELF

3. By finding remedial ways which make sense for people in customer service.

We will examine each of these in turn.

WHAT IS STRESS?

There are many definitions of stress, but a workable one you may find useful is 'a feeling of inability to cope when you think you ought to'. This can lead to:

- feeling on edge
- being overwhelmed by everything and out of control
- everything getting out of proportion
- not sleeping
- getting touchy at the slightest thing
- going off food or eating too much
- suffering stomach upsets
- having frequent colds or minor ailments
- accident proneness
- excess focusing on particular events or detail
- getting steamed up when you are delayed or late.

Stress is feeling you can't cope when you think you ought to.

Try going through this list and put a tick against those situations which currently apply to you. The more ticks the more likely you are to suffer from stress. Go through the list again for your team.

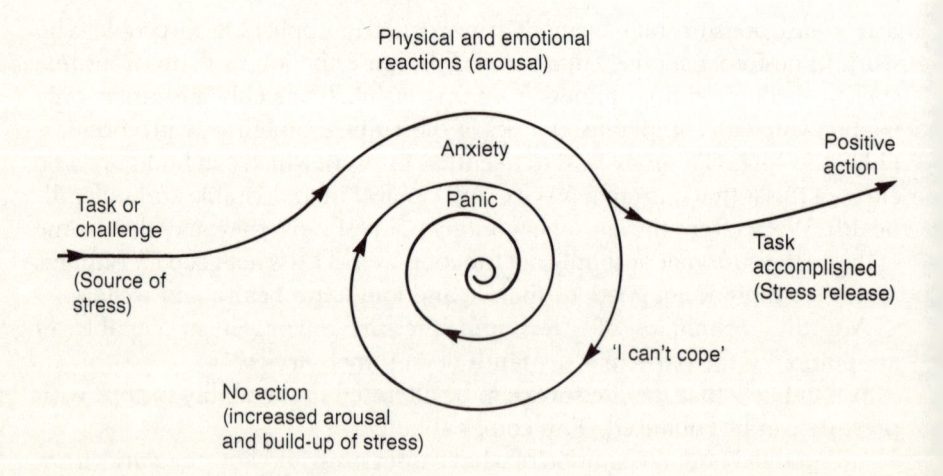

Figure 16.1 *How stress affects performance*

Stress is accompanied by a physical emergency response, thought to be nature's way of gearing us up to face immense danger or challenge in days gone by. Adrenalin and noradrenalin start pumping round, our stomach shuts down as blood is diverted to muscles, blood pressure rises, the heart beats faster and breathing is more rapid. This 'flight or fight' mechanism is involuntary.

So when does pressure become stress? The answer will vary from person to person but with pressure we may feel tired but not exhausted; we feel well able to cope and positive about the challenges we are facing. Our concentration is high, we keep things in perspective. Stress is a distorting and disabling illness. A certain amount of pressure is good for us – it stimulates us, it enables us to perform with energy and enthusiasm. Without it we would find ourselves becoming lethargic and would under-perform. Figure 16.1 shows how it can sometimes turn to stress.

SOME COMMON MYTHS

'It doesn't happen to me. Stress doesn't affect ordinary people'
Pressure affects many people in many occupations. It is a common factor in a customer service situation. Denial can lead to a build-up of stress. Be aware of changes and signals in your body and your feelings. Notice how you are feeling and pay attention to this: do not override the signals which tell you stress is apparent – the knotted stomach, the pounding heart, the tightness in your chest.

'You just keep going and shake it off'
You can ride through lower levels of short-term pressure. Developing good coping mechanisms rather than simply carrying on regardless will be more effective.

'Everyone is affected these days. You just have to put up with it'
True to some extent; there *is* a lot more stress than there used to be. But there is all the more reason consciously to take preventative action.

'A few drinks put me right'
This does not work – it just masks the symptoms. Taking an occasional drink can be good to help us unwind, as long as it is occasional and does not become excessive.

WILL YOU RUST OUT OR BURN OUT?

If you look at the curve illustrating how people behave under pressure in

Figure 16.2 you will see how pressure or stress affects us depending on how much we experience. At the lowest point we are under-stimulated and we under-perform – a condition sometimes called 'rust-out'. At the next stage we are performing well under the stimulation of pressure.

As we climb the curve of pressure there comes a point where we stop increasing our performance. We tip over into reduced performance. When we have gone beyond this optimum threshold point our performance starts to slip. This is when we are stressed. If we carry on like this when we are under some pressure or we encounter a sudden demand on us, our bodies move up a gear. This is a primitive response from days when we were hunters and gatherers and needed to fight or flee rapidly. Our brain signals 'red alert' and stress chemicals start pumping into the system.

In days gone by we would have eliminated these chemicals from our bodies by strong physical exertion and the body would return to its usual state. Today the threats may be an angry customer, worries about reorganisation or a difficult meeting. These chemicals hang around in our bodies and if we keep putting ourselves on alert we may find ourselves in a regular state of stress, physical and mental. Eventually, it is believed, this causes harm to our bodies – heart attacks, ulcers, even cancer are believed by many to have a stress link.

If we regularly push ourselves beyond our limits, our performance will get worse and we will eventually suffer a complete inability to continue.

If we regularly push ourselves beyond our limits, our performance will get worse and we will eventually suffer a complete inability to continue.

Each of us needs to know when we are reaching our pressure point which turns into stress. It is different for each one of us and in different circumstances.

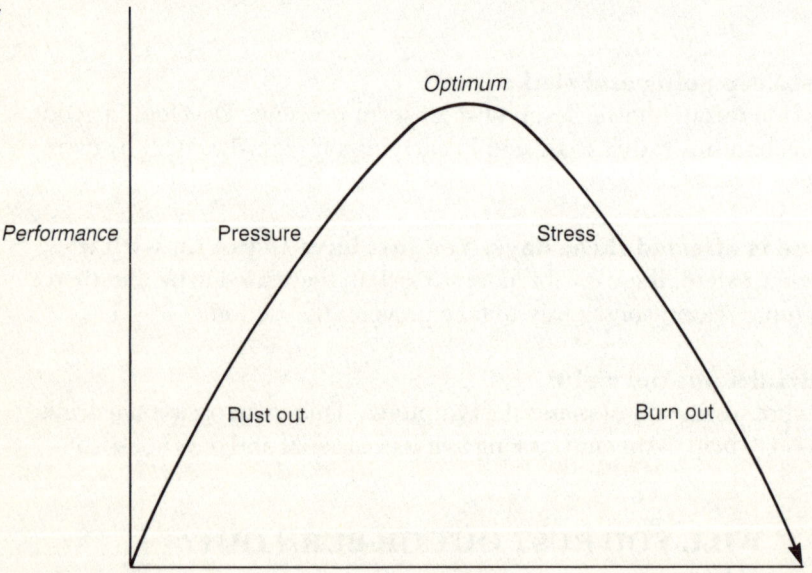

Figure 16.2 *How people behave under pressure*

A common problem in customer service situations is burn-out, that is people become exhausted and listless. This results from pushing yourself without let up and leads to a gradual wearing down. It can reach the point where you are barely functioning – you cease caring, you cease to find any enthusiasm for what you are doing.

HOW DO YOU SPOT STRESS?

As a manager you should look out for these signs of stress and follow up to check out your initial observations. Start with raising awareness of your own stress signs, perhaps by regular 'spot checks' on yourself at pre-determined intervals. The signs are:

- Noticeably more sickness and absenteeism, often apparently for quite normal reasons if taken by themselves – coughs and colds, sore throats, nasal trouble. It seems stress attacks our areas of physical weakness.
- Excessive perfectionism.
- Arguments or conflict with customers.
- Unusual conflict in the department or outside it.
- An increase in touchy or aggressive behaviour in the team or with customers.

Look out for signs of stress in yourself and your staff.

WHAT CAUSES STRESS?

Work overload
This is a common feature of many customer service activities. Less common today is work underload – not having enough to do, but this too is a cause of stress as time on one's hands seems to induce anxiety and a sense of worthlessness. Managers particularly need to make sure they do not suffer from keeping too many things to themselves and failing to delegate.

Change – too many new things at once
This may be a reorganisation, a change in procedures, a job change or changes in domestic circumstances like moving house, having builders in. They need not all be unwelcome changes either – even good things like promotion cause us stress initially.

Our personal make-up
Certain personality types are more vulnerable to stress. Work carried out in researching proneness to coronary heart disease suggests we can group people into personality types. One type is described as Type A. Type As:
- push themselves hard
- are competitive

Certain personality types are more vulnerable to stress than others.

- display impatience with themselves and other people
- put a lot of emphasis on success at work
- are always in a hurry.

These people are often in demand in customer service roles: they work hard and take their jobs very seriously. But there is a price to be paid and they are particularly prone to stress.

Type Bs on the other hand take life in a more relaxed way and do not get so het up and stressed. They are:
- relaxed about deadlines
- more concerned about quality than quantity of work
- slower in speech and movements.

Type ABs are able to respond flexibly as the situation demands. Why not complete the questionnaire in Table 16.1 and see which type you fit into?

Table 16.1 *Type A–type B behaviour*

Taking each pair of statements in turn, tick the number beside each statement which is most representative of your behaviour, 1 and 5 being closest to the different statements, 2 and 4 less close but still reflecting your behaviour. 3 is the middle between the two statements. Be honest with yourself: do not fill in the answers you feel you ought to.

Easy going about appointments	1	2	3	4	5	Never late
Not competitive	1	2	3	4	5	Plays to win
Listens carefully and hears people out	1	2	3	4	5	Interrupts, finishes other people's sentences
Rarely rushes or feels rushed	1	2	3	4	5	Always in a rush
Is patient while waiting	1	2	3	4	5	Cannot keep still while waiting
Takes one thing at a time	1	2	3	4	5	Juggles lots of things
Speaks slowly in a relaxed way	1	2	3	4	5	Speaks quickly, forcefully and with emphasis
Has own standards to judge good work	1	2	3	4	5	Seeks recognition from other people
Slow and deliberate	1	2	3	4	5	Rapid in everything
Easygoing	1	2	3	4	5	Drives hard
Expresses feelings	1	2	3	4	5	'Boils away' with feelings inside

Wide variety of interests – work is only one aspect of their lives	1	2	3	4	5	A workaholic – few interests outside work
Content to live for the moment	1	2	3	4	5	Always striving to get on and succeed
Easygoing in getting things done	1	2	3	4	5	Vigorous in making things happen

Scoring
Plot your total score by adding up the score of those you ticked. Then place your score according to the type as shown.

Type B	AB	Type A
1-14	15-42	43-77

What should you do about the consequences of your personality type? Particular attention should be paid to the Type A behaviour. Recent research suggests that the aggression component may be particularly damaging to the health of Type As. Aggression often shows itself at work in the form of severe competitiveness and time urgency, with never enough hours in the day. Type As need to:
- Be less aggressive
- Learn to slow down
- Listen to others and try to see their point of view
- Develop life outside work
- Manage their time better
- Reduce volume of work
- Relax and not take life so competitively and seriously.

Type Bs can be less concerned about the effects of stress, but they could usefully achieve more by setting themselves more stretching targets and being less of a perfectionist. Type Bs should be aware that they drive type As to distraction! Both types could usefully understand each other better.

DANGER! ARE YOU A WORKAHOLIC?

High workload plus the perfectionist, serious and over-conscientious personality can lead you to become a workaholic. Typical signs are:
- Inability to switch off from work problems or relax
- Dreaming about work
- Cancelling holidays because of work
- No friends outside work companions
- Frequently bringing work home, working weekends.

If you say yes to more than one of these, it is time you reassessed the balance between work and home. You are building up all the pre-conditions for stress. Look at yourself fairly and squarely. You may have been deceiving yourself saying 'It's only temporary, I'll slow down soon.'

Equally importantly, consider each of your team members to see whether

160 MANAGING YOURSELF

someone whom you may have overlooked or considered just conscientious is falling into this category.

How much time do you spend on the things that really give you pleasure?

The balance between work, home and leisure

Use Figure 16.3 to assess what gives you satisfaction. Now do the same for how much *time* in total you spend on all your activities. Is there a gap? What can you do about it? Divide up how much importance you attach to your interests, the things which satisfy you.

Example

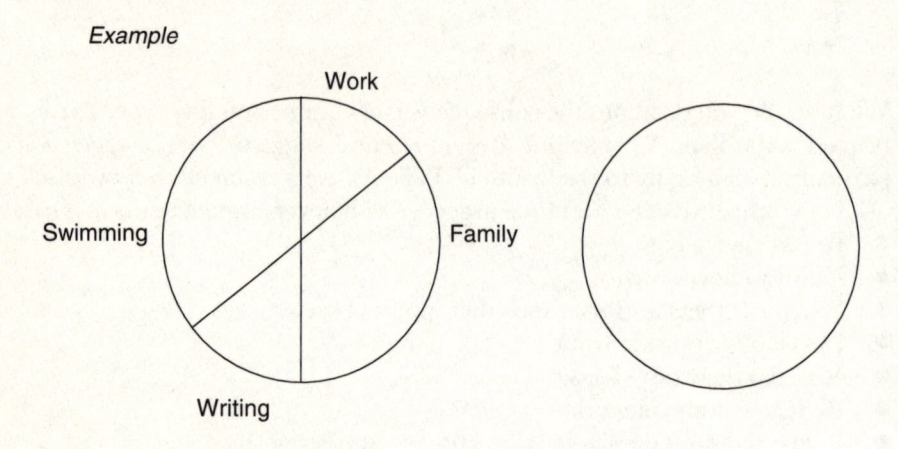

Figure 16.3 *Your circle of satisfaction*

POOR COPING STRATEGIES

Many people cope with stress in ways which do long-term harm, even though they appear to help in the short term. Examples are as follows.
- *Drinking*. This relieves the pressure for a while but then excess drink and dependency can start to bring their own problems.
- *Drugs*. Some people turn to tranquillisers only to find that they cannot come off them and the state they induce makes coping more difficult.
- *Cups of coffee and tea* to 'keep you going'. This will heighten your feelings of anxiety, though it may appear to give you a boost. Two or three cups of tea or coffee a day is about right for most people.
- *Smoking*. The long-term physical damage of smoking is now well proven – increased risk of heart disease, lung cancer and chest complaints.
- *Taking out your frustrations on other people* such as partners, friends, staff. This undermines any support you have and heightens a stressful atmosphere.

WHAT CAN MANAGERS DO ABOUT STRESS?

Managers should manage their own stress and do their best to minimise the harmful effects of stress on their staff, as follows:
- Keep an eye on the balance of workload. Is there anyone with more than they can cope with? Are you delegating enough?
- Introduce change with care. If possible ease in changes with careful planning and consultation – it will almost certainly be achieved more smoothly.
- Find ways to relax. The first thing that we often give up when we are busy is out-of-work activities, whereas in fact they should be the last. Physical exercise which you enjoy is good for taking your mind off work and helps burn off excess stress chemicals.
- Take a break and recharge the batteries. Keep up hobbies, whether they be going to the theatre or knitting.
- Use relaxation techniques.

    For example, find a quiet spot and get comfortable in a chair or lie down. Take a few deep breaths and exhale slowly. Concentrate on your breathing. Do this several times and consciously empty your mind of worries and thoughts by concentrating on this. Then focus your attention progressively on each part of your body, starting with your feet, then your legs and relax each of them like a rag doll.

    Alternatively think of a favourite spot in the country or the seaside. Imagine in detail being there and enjoying the sights and sounds and the pleasure of the situation.

    Imagine a meandering river. Picture writing each of the things you are concerned about on a piece of paper and watch them float away from you.
- If you spot stress in others, speak up supportively – do not ignore it.
- In a particularly heavy work period encourage people to take a short five minute break away from their work area at regular intervals and to take their full lunch breaks or take a breath of fresh air outside the building.
- Recognise the benefit of support networks, those groups of people on which we all need to off-load some of our worries, which may be made up of friends, colleagues, family. Generate the team as a supportive network for each other – we all need to let off steam after a difficult customer situation.
- When you know you are under pressure ask someone close to you, a colleague or partner, to give you a supportive reminder when you are going over the top and not coping well.
- Get adequate hours of sleep – nature's way to recharge your batteries. Make sure you get sufficient sleep to feel refreshed and do not start the day tired.
- Listen to a relaxation tape. There are a number on the market with soothing words and music. Be comfortable, loosen your clothing and give yourself a break. Unwinding mentally helps you to relax your body and to recharge yourself.
- Reduce unnecessary uncertainty and rumour. Keep people well informed. Give them some say in changes where possible.
- Give sufficient authority to your staff. Studies have shown this helps you and the customer – a problem is solved quickly instead of stress building up.

- Keep a stress diary as in Table 16.2 to recognise more accurately situations which stress you and your typical symptoms. This will allow you to be more sensitive to stress in yourself and anticipate potentially stressful situations.

Table 16.2 *Stress diary*

What happened	Stress rating of event (1 = low stress) (10 = explosive!)	Effects on you
Example Customer got angry with me	8	Stomach started churning. I felt panicky and upset

- Seek expert help – counsellors, doctors – if stress becomes regular and persistent. Many organisations are now more aware of stress, but it is still a subject that is not talked about enough. People are often unwilling to admit to feeling stressed. Create a climate where this is possible – from time to time it happens to us all in customer service.

SUMMARY

Good managers adopt these practices.
- Recognise pressure as a part of customer service. Stress builds up when the pressure is unrelenting and we do nothing about it.
- Notice and care for your staff. Know the symptoms and causes of stress.
- Keep a regular check on your stress level and take remedial action if it gets excessive.
- Encourage everyone to be aware of their own vulnerabilities and stress points.
- Use the team to work to each others' strengths and to support each other where each person is less strong.
- Recognise that different people cope differently and need support in areas which others find unstressful.
- Discourage regular work overload and long hours.

EXERCISES

1. Consider educating your staff in how to recognise and deal with stress. This is useful for themselves and also in recognising it in colleagues or customers.

2. If you are about to introduce changes, be aware of the rise in stress levels. Plan to spend time with each of your staff to deal with their concerns.
3. Check current workload and other stress factors. Are they excessive? If so, how will you deal with this to reduce stress levels?
4. Consider the benefits of an employee assistance programme, which involves confidential counselling, usually by an outsider, when employees are faced with personal or work-related issues which cause them stress and may hamper work performance.

◄ CONCLUSION ►

SEVEN ESSENTIALS FOR MANAGING SUPERIOR CUSTOMER SERVICE

This book offers practical guidelines for managing effectively in a customer service environment. Underlying these there are seven critical recommendations, outlined below. Putting these into action will empower your organisation to achieve an unrivalled level of service excellence.

1. Lead through customer-focused objectives

Agree team objectives which point toward the customer and are clear, measurable and realistic. Ensure that everyone knows what the team is aiming to achieve, and regularly review progress.

Make certain that in every activity you or your team undertake, you ask 'How will this improve the service we provide our customers?' Look at your organisation's procedures from a customer's perspective. Find out as much as possible about customers' needs and expectations. Remember, you have internal customers too.

2. Communicate your vision into action

You must have a vision, and communication makes the difference between vision and reality, carrying every member of your team towards commitment and vigorous action. Ensure that the verbal and non-verbal communication skills of you and your team match the messages you wish to convey.

A lot of success in communication is achieved through thorough, regular, painstaking effort. Ensure you follow a regular communications discipline by such means as meetings with your staff, colleagues and customers, newsletters, special events.

Keep talking and listening to your external customers, team members and internal customers. Act on what they tell you.

3. Build a powerful team – the basis for achieving customer success

You've recognised the crucial importance of teamwork, so select and build your team carefully. Ensure you involve your team members in decisions and encourage their active participation. Their combined contributions make the power for success. Delegate and give your people authority to take decisions and use their own judgement. Be proud of your team and show it. Encourage and guide your team members.

Gain commitment from others through your actions and behaviour. Personal example in dealing with customers is the best way to show the direction you want others to take.

4. Deploy your resources wisely

Make sure priorities are dictated by the customer, and then put your resources where they are going to make a difference.

Success lies in wisely putting resources where they will have most impact – and then keeping them that way as events change. Despite interruptions or crises, keep a steady eye on your priorities. Make sure you recognise the difference between importance and urgency. Allow contingency time for unexpected events.

5. Encourage a flexible and positive approach

Be flexible in your approach to problem solving. Do not always look for the solution which sticks by the book. Be prepared to listen and question and be creative in your approach.

Allow your people the room to be flexible in taking decisions affecting the customer – do not give them so little space to move that they and the customer feel frustrated.

Adopt an open and friendly manner in your dealings with both customers and the team. Be confident and positive in what you can offer. Recognise any shortcomings and work to overcome them.

6. Nurture and grow your people

An organisation really flourishes only if its people are growing. Recognise the power of training and development to equip and energise your staff to meet the current and future needs of your customers. Be mindful of the many ways to assist each individual to meet his or her development and career goals.

7. Ride on the crest of the wave of change

Use change positively as an opportunity for questioning everything and doing better. Fight change and you will go under. Work to the principles of regular improvement, and develop a plan of action to overcome areas of weakness. Review how you and your team are performing on a regular basis. Recognise and celebrate customer service success all along the way. Lots of small improvements can add up to a big change for the better.

◀ BIBLIOGRAPHY ▶

CHAPTER 1. CUSTOMER-FOCUSED LEADERSHIP

Adair, John (1983) *Effective Leadership*, Pan Books, London
Blanchard, Kenneth, Zigarmi, Patricia, and Zigarmi, Drea (1985) *Leadership and the One Minute Manager*, Fontana/Collins, London
Harvey-Jones, John (1988) *Making it Happen*, Fontana, London
Heim, Pat, and Chapman, Elwood (1990) *Learning to Lead*, Kogan Page, London
Pegg, Mike (1989) *Positive Leadership*, Mercury, London
Peters, Tom, and Austin, Nancy (1985) *A Passion for Excellence*, Fontana/Collins, London

CHAPTER 2. CREATING A POSITIVE IMAGE WITH CUSTOMERS

Brennan, Lynne, and Block, David (1991) *The Complete Book of Business Etiquette*, Piatkus, London
Davies, Philippa (1990) *Total Image: How to Communicate Success*, Piatkus, London

CHAPTER 3. HOW TO DEAL ASSERTIVELY WITH CUSTOMERS

Back, Ken and Kate (1982) *Assertiveness at Work*, McGraw-Hill, Maidenhead
Dickson, Ann (1986) *A Woman in your own Right*, Quartet Books, London
Lloyd, Sam, and Townsend, Anni (1991) *Developing Assertiveness*, Routledge, London

CHAPTER 4. MANAGING THE PROBLEM-SOLVING PROCESS

Brown, Mark (1992) *Successful Project Management in a Week*, Hodder & Stoughton, Sevenoaks
Pokras, Sandra (1989) *Systematic Problem Solving and Decision Making*, Kogan Page, London
Rawlinson, J Geoffrey (1989) *Creative Thinking and Brainstorming*, Gower, Aldershot

Townsend, John, and Farrier, Jacques (1990) *The Creative Manager's Pocketbook*, Management Pocketbooks, Alresford

CHAPTER 5. POSITIVE PERSUASION AND NEGOTIATION

Fisher, Roger, and Ury, William (1981) *Getting to Yes*, Arrow Books, London
Maddux, Robert (1988) *Successful Negotiation*, Kogan Page, London
Steele, Paul, Murphy, John, and Russell, Richard (1989) *It's a Deal*, McGraw-Hill, Maidenhead

CHAPTER 6. TOTAL QUALITY MANAGEMENT

Collard, Ron (1989) *Total Quality, Success Through People*, Institute of Personnel Management, London
Oakland, John (1991) *Total Quality Management*, Butterworth-Heinemann, Oxford

CHAPTER 7. DEALING WITH DIFFICULT CUSTOMER SITUATIONS

Cava, Roberta (1991) *Dealing with Difficult People*, Piatkus, London
Honey, Peter (1992) *Problem People and How to Manage Them*, Institute of Personnel Management, London
Ury, William (1991) *Getting Past No*, Business Books, London
Video Arts (1988) *From No to Yes, the Constructive Route to Agreement*, Video Arts Booklet, London

CHAPTER 8. COMMUNICATION AND GETTING THE MESSAGE ACROSS

Bone, Dave (1988) *A Practical Guide to Effective Writing*, Kogan Page, London
Decker, Bert (1988) *How to Communicate Effectively*, Kogan Page, London
Mandel, Steve (1988) *Effective Presentation Skills*, Kogan Page, London
Nierenberg, Gerard I, and Calero, Henry H (1973) *How to Read a Person Like a Book*, Thorsons, Wellingborough
Peel, Malcolm (1984) *Customer Service*, Kogan Page, London

CHAPTER 9. TEAMWORK

Adair, John (1986) *Effective Teambuilding*, Pan Books, London
Belbin, R Meredith (1991) *Management Teams*, Butterworth-Heinemann, Oxford
Hastings, Colin, Bixby, Peter, and Chaudhry-Lawton, Rani (1986) *Superteams*, Fontana/Collins, London
Maddux, Robert (1988) *Team Building*, Kogan Page, London

CHAPTER 10. RECRUITMENT AND SELECTION

Hodgson, Philip (1984) *A Practical Guide to Successful Interviewing*, McGraw-Hill, Maidenhead
Plumbley, Peter (1968) *Recruitment and Selection*, Institute of Personnel Management, London
Shackleton, Viv (1989) *How to Pick People for Jobs*, Fontana/Collins, London

CHAPTER 11. PERFORMANCE MANAGEMENT

Blanchard, Kenneth, and Johnson, Spencer (1983) *The One Minute Manager*, Fontana/Collins, London
Hudson, Howard (1992) *The Perfect Appraisal*, Century Business, London
King, Patricia (1984) *Performance Planning and Appraisal*, McGraw-Hill, New York

CHAPTER 12. TRAINING AND DEVELOPMENT

Harrison, Rosemary (1992) *Employee Development*, Institute of Personnel Management, London
Honey, Peter, and Mumford, Alan (1982) *The Manual of Learning Styles*, Honey, Maidenhead
Rae, Leslie (1983) *The Skills of Training: a Guide for Managers and Practitioners*, Gower, Aldershot

CHAPTER 13. THE INTERNAL CUSTOMER

Video Arts (1989) *An Inside Job*, Video Arts Booklet, London
Wyvern Business Training (1992) *Internal Customer*, Wyvern, Ely

CHAPTER 14. DEVELOPING YOURSELF

Francis, Dave (1985) *Managing your own Career*, Fontana/Collins, London
Harris, Thomas A (1967) *I'm OK, you're OK*, Pan Books, London
Hopson, Barrie, and Scally, Mike (1984) *Build your own Rainbow*, Mercury, London
Pedler, Mike, Burgoyne, John, and Boydell, Tom (1978) *A Manager's Guide to Self Development*, McGraw-Hill, Maidenhead
Woodcock, Mike, and Francis, Dave (1982) *The Unblocked Manager*, Gower, Aldershot

CHAPTER 15. TIME MANAGEMENT

Hayes, Marion (1987) *Make Every Minute Count*, Kogan Page, London
Noon, James (1985) *'A' Time*, Van Nostrand Reinhold (UK), Wokingham
Seiwart, Lothar J (1989) *Managing your Time*, Kogan Page, London

CHAPTER 16. MANAGING UNDER PRESSURE

Cranwell-Ward, Jane (1987) *Managing Stress*, Pan Books, London
Froggatt, Helen, and Stamp, Paul (1991) *Managing Pressure at Work*, BBC Books, London
Hanson, Peter (1988) *The Joy of Stress*, Pan Books, London
Rudinger, Edith (1988) *Understanding Stress*, Consumers' Association, London
Watts, Murray, and Cooper, Cary (1991) *Relax: Dealing with Stress*, BBC Books, London

… INDEX ▶

achievement, recognition of 109
aggression
   coping with 30–1, 60–1
   in relation to assertiveness 27–8
answering the telephone 21–2
appearance 20
appraisals and performance reviews 106–7
assertiveness 27–34
   acknowledging feelings 29–30
   assumptions necessary for 29
   benefits of 28–9
   and body language 30
   coping with different situations 30–1
   defined 27
   feelings 29–30
   a short guide to 29
   summary 31–2
   exercises 32–4
attitude surveys 36
   external 75
   internal 36, 129
awards 109
awareness
   of self 133
   of others 137

bad news, giving customers 61
barriers to doing business 54
behaviour change 107–8
Belbin team roles 83–5
benefits vs. features 45
body language 30, 70–2
brainstorming 38–9
burnout 155–7

chairing meetings and discussions 73–4, 124
change 166
   and learning 118–20
checklists
   company image 24–6
   leadership 14–15
   personal improvement 139–40
communication 64–79
   at meetings 73–4
   and body language 30, 70–2
   giving clear explanations 70
   listening 68–9
   maintaining 75–6
   making presentations 74–5
   preparation for 67
   on the telephone 21–2, 72

172 INDEX

    tips for smooth-flowing 67–8
    why is it so difficult? 65–6
    written 21, 72–3
    summary 77
    exercises 77–9
company image checklist 24–6
complaints, customer 58–9
conflict, strategies for handling 43–4
    dealing with aggression 60–1
    team conflict 86–7
cooperation, in teams 86
creativity 38–9
crisis management 148
criticism
    receiving 58–9
    giving 104–5
customer interface, managing the 11–62
    assertiveness 27–34
    creating a positive image 19–26
    customer feedback 75, 76, 129
    customer-focused leadership 12–18
    customer friendliness 55–6
    difficult customer situations 57–62
        dealing with aggression 60–1
        giving bad news 61
        handling complaints 58–9
        is the customer always right? 61–2
        saying 'no' 62
        typical encounters 59–60
        summary 62
        exercises 62
    positive persuasion and negotiation 42–50
    the problem-solving process 35–41
    seven essentials for 164–6
    total quality management 51–6

decision-making, evaluating options for 39–40
delegation 150–1
development, personal 115, 132–41
    defined 133
    feeling positive 137–8
    getting feedback 134–5
    how OK are you? 135–6
    the Johari window 133–4
    self-awareness and development 138–40
    summary 140
    exercises 141
development plan 116
difficult customer situations 57–62

eighty/twenty rule 148–9
exercises
    assertiveness 32–4
    creating an image 26
    difficult customer situations 62
    the internal customer 130
    performance management 110–11
    persuasion and negotiation 50
    problem-solving 41
    recruitment and selection 96–7
    self-development 141
    stress management 162–3
    time management 151–2
    training and development 125
explanation giving 70

face-to-face communication 70–1
feedback, giving 104, 105
feelings, the assertive approach to 29–30
fishbone diagrams 38–9

goals 101
goodwill 21
groups 80–1

ideas 38–9
I'm OK, you're OK 135–7
image, creating an 19–26
    building up an image 20–1
    company image checklist 24–6
    image defined 19–20
    social relations with customers 23–4
    on the telephone 21–2, 72
    tips 22–3

INDEX

use of names 22
written communications 21
summary 26
exercises 26
incentives and rewards 109-10
induction training 115
influencing
  persuasion and negotiation 40-50
  assertiveness 27-34
interaction 127-9
internal customer, the 126-30
  defined 126-7
  providing a good service to 127-9
  quality of service to 127
  summary 129-30
  exercises 130
interviewing
  alternatives 95
  do's and don'ts 94-5
  pitfalls 92-4
  preparation 90-2
  questions 94
involvement 51-3

job descriptions 91
Johari window, the 133-4

key result areas 100-1

leadership
  customer-focused 12-18
    developing leadership skills 15
    increasing effectiveness 17-18
    leadership checklist 14-15
    managing and leadership 13
  resourceful team 63-130
    communication 64-79
    the internal customer 126-30
    performance management 98-111
    recruitment and selection 89-97
    teamwork 80-8
    training and development 112-25

learning 120
letter writing 72-3
listening, active 68-9

management
  of the customer interface 11-62
  performance 98-111
  total quality 51-6
  of yourself 131-63
  vs leadership 13-14
    developing yourself 132-41
    time management 142-52
    under pressure 153-63
Maslow's theory of motivation 103
measurement
  a principle of TQM 52
  of objectives 101
meetings
  being assertive at 31
  communication at 73-4
  making presentations 74-5
  performance review 106-7
  and teamwork 87
morale 36, 129
motivation and performance 85, 102-4

names, use of 22
negotiation 47-50
'no', saying 62
non-verbal communication 70-1

objectives, setting 101
OK-not OK 135-7
open questions 94

performance management 98-111
  benefits customer service 99-100
  defined 98-9
  giving feedback 104-5
  key result areas 100-1
  making it work in practice 101-2
  motivation and performance 102-4

performance review meetings 106-7
reward and incentive methods 109-10
setting objectives 101
strategies for individual 107-9
summary 110
exercises 110-11
personal improvement checklist 139-40
personality, type A and type B 157-9
persuasion and negotiation 42-50
   how to be persuasive 45-6
   negotiating 47-9
   power of the positive approach 46-7
   strategies 43-4
   tips on negotiation 49
   summary 50
   exercises 50
plans
   coaching 122
   delegation 150
   time 149
   training 116
   using charts 38
poor performance 107
positive approach 44, 137-8
praise, giving 105
presentations, making 74-5
pressures, effects of 155-7
priority setting 148-9
problem-solving
   encouraging people 36-7
   indicators of ineffective 35-6
   methods for identifying and solving problems 38-40
   a systematic approach to 37-8
   summary 40-1
   exercises 41
procedures, customer friendly 54-6
project
   for development 122-3
   management
psychometric tests 95

quality 51-3
questioning 94
questionnaires
   listening 68-9
   teamwork 82
   training and development 114
   type A-type B behaviour 158-9
   use of 9, 12, 36, 75

recognition 104-5, 109-110
recruitment and selection 89-97
   interview pitfalls 92-6
   selecting candidates 89-90
   the stages in 90-2
   summary 96
   exercises 96-7
responsibilities
   definition 100
   for training 112
   of a leader 12-17
   of a team leader 85-6
reviews, performance 106
rewards 109-110

saying 'no' 62
self-development, encouraging 115
self-image 135-7
social relations with customers 23-4
   opportunities for 23-4
   preparation for 24
   wining and dining 23
standards in TQM 52
   service standards 23
stress 153-63
   causes of 157-9
   defined 154-5
   how to spot 157
   poor coping strategies 160
   rust or burn out? 155-7
   some common myths 155
   what managers can do about 161-2
   workaholics 159-60

summary 162
exercises 162–3
success, celebration 109–110
surveys
   customer 75
   internal 36, 129
SWOT analysis 141

teamwork 80–8, 165
   at meetings 87
   balance in a team 83–5
   benefits of 81
   improving a service team 86–7
   lack of 81
   questionnaire 82–3
   role of team leader 85–6
   in a service environment 80
   tips 88
   summary 87
telephone image 21–2, 72
time management 142–52
   applying strategy to good service 146–51
   common objections to 142–4
   recognising bad habits 144–6
   time wasters 147–8
   summary 151
   exercises 151–2
total quality management 51–6
   the beneficiaries of 52
   defined 51–2
   the principles of 52–3
   procedures 54–5
   some TQM questions and answers 53–4
   tips for greater customer friendliness 55–6
   summary 56
   exercises 56
training and development 112–25
   coaching 119–22
   discussions 124
   encouraging self-development 115
   evaluation and follow up 124
   how people learn 118–19
   induction training 115
   need for a systematic approach 115–18
   options 118
   projects 122–3
   some objections to 113–14
   training course 123–4
   summary 124–5
   exercises 125
type A, type B behaviour 158–9

user friendliness 54–6

win/win 47–9
wining and dining 23
writing to customers 21, 72–3